The New Americans
Recent Immigration and American Society

Edited by
Steven J. Gold and Rubén G. Rumbaut

A Series from LFB Scholarly

The Criminalization of Immigration
The Post 9/11 Moral Panic

Samantha Hauptman

LFB Scholarly Publishing LLC
El Paso 2013

Copyright © 2013 by LFB Scholarly Publishing LLC

All rights reserved.

Library of Congress Cataloging-in-Publication Data

Hauptman, Samantha.
  The criminalization of immigration : the post 9/11 moral panic /
Samantha Hauptman.
      pages cm. -- (The New Americans : Recent Immigration and
American Society)
  Includes bibliographical references and index.
  ISBN 978-1-59332-616-6 (hardcover : alk. paper)
  1. United States--Emigration and immigration--Government policy. 2.
Immigration enforcement--United States 3. Illegal aliens--United
States. 4. War on Terrorism, 2001-2009. I. Title.
  JV6483.H375 2013
  325.73--dc23
                                2013000005

ISBN 978-1-59332-616-6

Printed on acid-free 250-year-life paper.

Manufactured in the United States of America.

Dedication

For my husband Ryszard - and to think that this idea began with
that impromptu afternoon drive to Cherokee

Table of Contents

List of Tables

List of Figures

CHAPTER 1

Introduction

While the study of terrorism had previously been neglected by sociologists (Deflem 2004a; Turk 2004), since the attacks on September 11th 2001, the "war on terror" has increased the public's awareness of the potential for foreign threats against American society (Bonn 2011; Engel 2004; Haque 2003; Kettl 2004; Klinger and Grossman 2002; McKenzie 2004; Rothe & Muzzatti 2004; Saux 2007; Scheuerman 2002; Wanta, Golan, & Lee 2004; Welch 2006a). The United States "war on terror" was initiated on September 20th, 2001, when President George W. Bush described a "new kind of war... [that has] raised new issues for how to treat those involved in... as well as those associated with the war on the United States" (Kettl 2004: 98). A new kind of war with the U.S. refers to the long-term threat of terrorism that had thus become one of the Bush Administration's primary focal point, and has continued to capture the public's attention, with issues of national security and immigration as the leading concerns.

As the federal response to terrorism was being formulated, the unprecedented breadth and magnitude of the government's decree also began to materialize. The need for an appropriate response to the terrorist acts against the U.S. was not only evident but also considered essential to preserve the security of the country. In fact, "the extraordinary threat of modern terrorism has been mirrored by extraordinary counter measures" (Turk 2004: 281; Ackerman 2004), which are directly revealed by the passage of the USA PATRIOT Act (Uniting and Strengthening America by Providing Appropriate Tools Required to Intercept and Obstruct Terrorism Act of 2001). Hence, the Bush administration's declaration of the "war on terror" was officially galvanized with the passage of the USA PATRIOT Act on October 26, 2001.

With new federal ancillary investigative powers, the USA PATRIOT Act (hereafter the PATRIOT Act or the Act) has far-reaching consequences, affecting both citizens and non-citizens alike. Although its primary enterprise centers on vastly increasing funding to virtually all aspects of law enforcement (Collins 2002); investigative tools, information sharing, new technology, and increased penalties are the main components that further enhance the ability of the U.S. government to "prevent, investigate, and prosecute acts of terror" (*United States Department of Justice* 2001). Each of these components is not only funded by the provisions of the PATRIOT Act, but also enforced by a wide support system including federal, state, and local agencies, that collaborate to share the responsibility of protecting the country. With a heightened awareness of terrorism and an increased concern for national security, the PATRIOT Act therefore functions as the federal government's primary form of social control. The expanded authority effectively raises the awareness of terrorism, but also imposes increased government enforcement, surveillance, and even suspicion against virtually all segments of society.

In order to sustain the PATRIOT Act's overall directive, the federal government's rhetoric must routinely and publicly respond to "huge budgetary commitments to homeland security, to the intelligence serves, and to the Pentagon, as well as to raised concerns about infringements on basic liberties" (Falk 2003: 216). Opponents of the PATRIOT Act assert that these security measures have raised the level of fear and suspicion toward foreigners and immigration in post 9/11 society while conspicuously curtailing the civil rights and liberties previously afforded to both citizens and non-US citizens (Chang 2002; Heymann 2002; Saux 2007; Welch 2003).

Given the federal governments firm stance on homeland security and the diverse group of challengers that are critical of the new immigration restrictions, these two opposing forces have therefore made the Act a well-publicized and familiar subject of debate among the general public. It may therefore be evident that, with an increased awareness of the flaws in the federal immigration system and subsequent national security issues (Ashar 2002; Diaz 2011; Hall 2002; Lebowitz and Podheiser 2002;), the PATRIOT Act's legally imposed restrictions on immigrants and visitors to America have caused a moral panic, inadvertently leading to the criminalization of immigrants in the post-September 11th era.

THE CONCEPT OF MORAL PANICS

The notion of moral panics was introduced by Jock Young (1971) in a late 1960s study that observed the sudden and escalating public reaction to drug abuse, during a period of increased law enforcement and arrests in Britain. The moral panic expression, referring to an event that occurs in under particular social conditions, marries two terms where moral refers to a righteous or just social order and panic is denoted as a crisis or sudden change, causing turmoil or distress in society (Thompson 1998). The expression moral panics therefore implies that an occurrence, perceived as a threat to society, has the potential to critically change social values, norms, and regulations and that its occasion may vitally disrupt the sanctity of society.

As the occurrence of a moral panic causes an unexpected, fundamental change at the very essence of society, it is also likely that what results are "a demand for greater social regulation or control and a demand for a return to 'traditional' values'" (Thompson 1998: 8-9). With this rationalization, the moral panic conception includes several other components that further justify and explain an incident as it escalates throughout all facets of society, thus contributing to and formally defining a moral panic environment. Given the distinct character of a moral panic atmosphere, it is necessary to further define the notions of social control and deviance as they relate to the moral panic conception and explain the significance of two main sociological frameworks that are considered relevant: law and collective action (Cohen 1972: 11). Nevertheless, first evident in a moral panic environment is the modification of both formal and informal social control mechanisms.

THE CONCEPT OF SOCIAL CONTROL

Goode and Ben-Yehuda (1994) assert that societies may experience moral panics, which are formally distinguished as reactions to various events in society, from the media, public, and most notably from social control agents. In this context, social control agents refer to two distinct systems of social control in society, including formal and informal mechanisms that develop to regulate the conduct of individuals and assure conformity to existing rules or laws (Quinney 1970: 36). The distinction between formal and informal social controls is imperative in the moral panic environment as each type's role fluctuates, as their overall effect and influence assists in determining the extent of the panic.

Formal Social Control

Formal social controls include all aspects of a society's criminal justice system. Officially sanctioned laws and legislation, police and law enforcement agencies, and judicial systems with a corresponding prescribed set of punishments, function within society to impose formal social controls. Therefore, each agency serves to ensure "that norms are followed and the social order remains unchallenged… [and] normative violations do not threaten the social order" (Goode and Ben-Yehuda 1994: 76). Formal social controls are therefore not dictated or determined by a single individual but rather from several individuals in society where their "efforts tend to represent, reflect, and grow out of the views and concerns of groups which they represent or to which they belong" (Ibid. 1994: 81).

Formal social control agents in society refer to two interconnected groups, rule creators and rule enforcers, collectively distinguished as moral entrepreneurs (Becker 1969: 147). Rule creators are defined as:

> Specifically, lawmakers, politicians, and other inside players involved in the legislation process [that] provide the legal justification for law-enforcement campaigns. Through legislation, rule creators legitimize authority whereby the state increases its power to monitor and regulate the conduct of its citizens. (Welch 2000: 110)

Consequently, it is the rule creators in society that designate particular types of conduct as beyond the accepted or established norms; in effect, labeling behavior as deviant or criminal (Goode and Ben-Yehuda 1994). As rule creators establish laws and legislation to address deviation from social norms, the rule enforcers must then implement official guidelines to ensure that the regulations imposed on society are adhered to. The rule enforcers must therefore include all groups associated with the implementation of laws, including the judicial system, police, and law enforcement officials and agencies (Ibid. 1994).

Moral entrepreneurs do not act alone or independent of the social order. In a given society, they must be guided by the prevailing attitudes or concerns of the general public they represent (Goode and Ben-Yehuda 1994). Hence, once a social problem or concern develops among the general public, moral entrepreneurs begin the task of publicly addressing the problem though law and the enforcement of new legislation, designed to directly manage or attend to the perceived social problem. In this capacity, moral entrepreneurs concurrently take on the role of "claims making", identified as they "contribute to public anxiety by publicizing false or exaggerated claims about the putative problem, often by generating and disseminating statistics and figures"(Welch et al. 2002: 16).

Dictated by the existing social climate, moral entrepreneurs publicly address and expose social concerns as a constant enterprise. In a panic environment, their auxiliary activity includes "amplifying deviance and orchestrating social reactions so the panic becomes a consensus-generating envoy for the dominant ideology" (Ibid. 2001: 284). In effect, with access to and influence on formal social controls, moral entrepreneurs as claims makers have a major role in inciting, advancing, and conceivably sustaining a moral panic environment.

Informal Social Control

Although official policies and standards are adhered to as formal means of social control, there are also informal influences that contribute greatly to an individual's level of compliance to social control mechanisms. In fact, "when it comes to forcing conformity of belief and behavior, government coercion takes a back seat to private, social pressure...In matters of opinion, whether by fashion or opinion, we tend to believe what others around us believe, not what the government tries to force us to believe" (Gellman 2002: 89). With government influence playing a secondary role, it then becomes the informal social control mechanisms that lead individuals in formulating opinions and guiding values and beliefs. Further, informal controls working in conjunction with formal social controls direct citizens to accept socially prescribed norms and conform to the prevailing laws enacted by moral entrepreneurs (Ibid: 89).

With the combined facets of the criminal justice system, formal social controls include:

> Highly formalized institutions of the state... [which collectively] produces a generalized belief system – mythologies, stigmas, stereotypes – but also produces or tries to produce new methods of control... [with] the

ultimate formalization being achieved when new laws are actually created. (Cohen 1972: 111)

Correspondingly, informal social control mechanisms include all other social influences, "not officially sanctioned by the state or any other recognized authority" (Welch 2000: 95). Although not official, informal controls are equally as influential and important to the discovery of social concerns or problems and contribution to each individual's general perception of social norms.

Although no established or officially defined guidelines exist for informal control mechanisms:

> Social control is a normative aspect of social life... found wherever and whenever people hold each other to standards, explicitly or implicitly, consciously or not: on the street, in prison, at home, at a party. It divides people into those who are respectable and those who are not; it disgraces some, but protects the reputations of others. (Black 1976: 105)

Essentially, in order to induce conformity, informal social control agents are compelled to distinguish a concern or particular designee(s) as opposing collective norms, allowing formal agents to follow by initiating official measures that address public concerns and regulate all forms of deviation from socially accepted norms.

Moreover, when any form of social control is manifested as a response to publicly induced, society changing actions, they should be considered as a, "dynamic factor or 'cause' of deviation" (Lemert 1964: 97), since control mechanisms effectively label the object of control as a source of deviance or criminality. This is one of the main attributes of social control as the public's concern or understanding of social problems "in complex modern societies seldom develops as a straightforward upsurge of indignation... - there is a 'politics of social problems'

or to put it another way, they are 'socially constructed'."
(Thompson 1998: 12).

THE SOCIAL CONSTRUCTION OF DEVIANCE

Social control refers, "broadly to virtually all of the human
practices and arrangements that contribute to the social order
and, in particular, that influence people to conform... [and] more
narrowly to how people define and respond to deviant behavior"
(Black 1998: 4). Socially defined deviance is therefore
dependent on the level of influence both formal and informal
social control mechanisms have on a society, and varies in
accordance with the reigning social norms, ideological outlook,
and cultural value systems (Davis and Anderson 1983: 13). As
part of the social order then, deviant or criminal pretense,
whether committed against an individual or society as a whole, is
dependent on and subject to both formal and informal social
controls.   Hence, in any given social order, deviance is not
inherently defined; "it is created by society" (Becker 1969: 8).

Kitsuse (1962) asserts that deviance is a process where
members of society interpret, define, and suitably respond to
deviant behavior (p. 248), in accordance with the "responses of
the conventional and conforming members of the society who
identify and interpret behavior as deviant" (p. 253). This notion
epitomizes the influencing role of moral entrepreneurs in society
where even as a group or individual may not in fact be guilty of
deviant behavior, they may still be socially defined as deviant. It
is therefore evident that "the formal approach to regulating
deviance leads to the criminalizing of undesirable conduct, and
precisely which behaviors are criminalized is subject to an array
of social forces" (Welch 2000: 115). These social forces include
the combination of formal social control implementations,
endorsed by informal social control mechanisms.

As formal social control agents, moral entrepreneurs take the
primary role in defining and establishing social norms for the
rest of society, based on the prevailing social climate. Given
their official capacity, moral entrepreneurs therefore have the

ability to provide most effective means of precipitating lasting social changes, by lawfully defining what is socially acceptable, or conversely, redefining what is considered deviant. In fact:

> Nowhere is the contingent nature of deviation made more apparent in our society than in the action of government regulatory agencies with adjudicative and punitive powers in situations where they are confronted by consequences of technological and organizational change... [where] the real source of deviation in such areas is not necessarily change in the behavior of the subjects of regulation, but may be the imposition of new rules which define existing behavior, or behavior consistent with older norms, as now deviant. The object of defining the behavior is to produce change, not to repress it. (Lemert 1964:91)

It is therefore a society's social control agents that take an active role, changing society as they "advance or defend their values, define deviation and also assign deviant acts to individuals. This frequently, or characteristically in our society, reflects choice, valuation, and group interaction" (Lemert 1964: 97). With carefully constructed, socially defined deviance secured, informal social control mechanisms further advance deviant designations by conveying and affirming these labels to the rest of society.

As a basic premise of labeling theory, labels that define an event, and eventually determine an appropriate response, are created or assigned by society; a process also referred to as societal reaction theory (Newman 2003: 219). Therefore, as social problems are formally identified and deviant labels are established, the application of social control procedures is executed (Cullen 1984: 125), resulting in a general public reaction to alleged deviance.

The influence of labels created by society, is evident as informal controls become a more apparent, "consequence of the

application by others of rules and sanctions to an 'offender'"
(Becker 1969: 8-9); thus publicly labeling a particular individual
or group as deviant or potentially deviant. Lemert and Winter
(2000) further extend the notion of labeling by asserting that:

> [T]here is a progressive reciprocal relationship between
> the deviation of the individual and the societal reaction,
> with a compounding of the societal reaction out of the
> minute accretions in the deviant behavior, until a point is
> reached where in grouping and out grouping between
> society and the deviant is manifest. At this point a
> stigmatizing of the deviant occurs in the form of name
> calling, labeling, or stereotyping. (p. 38)

Once social stigmatization has occurred as a consequence of
social controls, individuals or groups labeled as deviant are
openly affirmed as potential offenders or outsiders in society. It
is at this point that "deviance can be made explicit by saying that
human beings and their actions may become objects or subjects
of disapproval, condemnation, penalties, ostracism, banishment,
segregation, treatment, and unsolicited help or even friendly
advice - that is, of social controls" (Lemert and Winter 2000:
63).

The control or regulation of society therefore deals with
deviance and resultant criminality as society becomes,
"characterized by two interlocking and mutually conditioning
patterns of action: the formal controls exercised by the state's
criminal justice agencies and the informal social controls that are
embedded in the everyday activities and interactions of civil
society" (Garland 2001: 5). More concisely, social controls are
an effective tactic for the management of socially constructed
deviance in society, achieved through the implementation of law
and the subsequent overt and widespread criminalization of
suspected deviant social groups.

LAW AND CRIMINALIZATION

In any social order, "it is presumed that criminal law is a reflection of society's moral code" (Welch 2000: 115). Therefore, a legal strategy becomes evident as public concern is generated about a particular state of society and causes a battle, waged against a specific individual or group, resulting in "the creation of a new fragment of the moral constitution of society, its code of right and wrong" (Becker 1969: 145); most often legitimized by the establishment of laws. The formalization of new laws: "can thus be seen as symbolizing the public affirmation of social ideals and norms as well as a means of direct social control" (Gusfield 1967: 177). As adjustments in both the social and legal system are observed, criminalization therefore occurs in the form of changes to universally held social norms and the modification of related laws.

In this study, criminalization is defined as, "the socialization of individuals into crime and the legislative/administrative process by which human actions are defined as criminal and those committing them subjected to social control" (Lemert and Winter 2000: 263). The notion of criminalization in a given society may therefore be characterized as the public response to socially defined deviance resulting from the official labeling and enactment of laws that define deviance or criminality. In effect, "in the modern world, law has become the paramount agency of social control" (Pound [1942] 1997: 20) that "rests upon the power or force of politically organized society" (Ibid: 49).

As the enactment of new laws often provides a foundation for the, "denial of various civil rights to certain social and political minority groups, religious groups, racial and ethnic groups, and political dissenters of various persuasion" (Quinney 1970: 60), new legislation may effectively criminalize and/or endorse the criminalization of particular individuals and social groups. Given this notion of formal criminalization, it is assumed that as some groups are suspected of being guided by values that are different from the prevailing value system, their motives and intentions become suspected as deviant or even criminal to the rest of society (Ibid: 60).

With law as a form of social control, designed to influence, constrain, and deter "conduct at variance with the postulates of social order" (Pound [1942] 1997: 18), an important focus of law then becomes preserving the security and functioning of the social order, against any conduct that is deemed a threatening or against collective social interests (Pound 1943: 20-21). Therefore, once social controls establish conditions that are conducive to the preservation and protection of the social order, further recognition of potential harm may be evident with the assistance of additional groups that are fuelled by collective action.

THEORETICAL FRAMEWORK OF MORAL PANICS

The moral panic environment may be characterized as a multifaceted assemblage of reactions to social conditions or problems, involving the media, the public, and various agents of social control (Goode and Ben-Yehuda 1994; Welch 2000). The panic is not unbounded but instead is instigated by a general public concern over socially defined norms, perceived as deviance (Ben-Yehuda 2009; Welch 2000). Then, as the concern gains prominence it is amplified as an escalating social concern or problem warranting a solution that in turn, is sought by mobilizing a response and appropriate resources to quell the panic (Welch 2000).

In these cases, "the mass media, pressure groups, politicians, sections of the public, the police and the judiciary" (Thompson 1998: 9) combine to further fuel the panic. A moral panic episode can therefore only be sustained as its escalation and dispersal in a given society persist, through the collective action of various facets of society, the existence of *folk devils*, and the impact of the media.

Collective Action

In moral panics, the notion of collective action is marked by; "mass hysteria, delusion and panics, and also a body of studies on how societies cope with sudden threat or disorder caused by physical disasters" (Cohen 1972: 11). With the perception of deviance as a society-defined creation, it follows that members of society collectively establish social rules that are considered moral regulations. Moral panics are evident as they become, "a [palpable] kind of fever; it can be characterized by heightened emotion, fear, dread, anxiety, hostility, and a strong feeling of righteousness" (Goode and Ben-Yehuda 1994: 31).

Thus, moral panics are a reaction to "symptoms or signs of struggle over rival discourses and regulatory practices" (Thompson 1998: 30) and what is considered unacceptable to a society as a whole, potentially leading to the elevation of the level of suspicion against anyone or anything associated as a threat. In moral panics, threats must therefore include some incarnation of *folk devils*.

The Threat of *Folk Devils*

Moral panics advocate the belief of *folk devils*, where an identifiable person or group of people to concentrate upon is essential. The notion of *folk devils* allows the public to focus their perceived threat on a specific category of deviants that can be both named and identified. In effect, "these perpetrators or supposed perpetrators come to be regarded as the enemy - or an enemy - of society…deviants, outsiders, legitimate and deserving targets of self-righteous anger, hostility, and punishment" (Goode and Ben-Yehuda 1994: 31). In fact:

> [T]he key ingredient in the emergence of a moral panic is the creation or intensification of hostility toward and denunciation of a particular group, category, or cast of characters. The emergence or reemergence of a deviant category characterizes the moral panic; central in this

process is the targeting of new or past "folk devils."
(Ibid. 1994: 74)

The discovery of this group actually becomes part of the moral panic and is consequently, associated with or identified as a threatening or harmful to the sanctity of society.

Media Influence and Effect

The final and perhaps most important component of moral panic is the assistance of the media, frequently encouraging the spread and promotion of moral crises in society (Bonn 2011; Cohen 1972; Goode and Ben-Yehuda 1994; McRobbie and Thornton 1995; Thompson 1998; Young 2009). Especially true today, the media are able to reach its audience at all times and in virtually all places. Although the media's primary occupation is to inform of events that are entertaining, enlightening, and perhaps relevant to the safety and security of the audience, they have habitually played an active role in promoting moral panics. Adding to the fury and proliferation, the media are capable of presenting seemingly small events or episodes and thrusting them into an individual's consciousness, by means of a reinterpretation of seemingly mundane behavior or actions, which are then abruptly deemed deviant (Cohen 1972: 77); this is the essence of media sensitization.

At various times the mass media has, served as "agents of indignation…[in] their very reporting of certain 'facts' [which] can be sufficient to generate concern, anxiety, indignation or panic" (Cohen 1972: 16). Therefore, even inadvertently, media sensitization may create its own *folk devils*, by reporting that a, "group or category engages, or is said to engage, in unacceptable, immoral behavior, presumably causes or is responsible for serious harmful consequences, and is therefore seen as a threat to the well-being, basic values, and interests of the society presumably threatened by them" (Goode and Ben-Yehuda 1994: 31). A moral panic environment can therefore be sustained as:

The media possesses the ability to influence public opinion. As a result, it remains on the 'front lines in the state's battle to formulate a sense of cohesive purpose and national identity...political and corporate elites often take great strides to ensure their agenda is supported by the mainline media. (Welch 2003: 14)

In fact, the tendency of the media toward exaggeration and sensationalism is most evident in the moral panic environment.

Also included in media reporting is predicting future events that stimulate the public's reaction. The media frequently focuses reporting on stories that are sensational, scandalous, or bizarre, essentially broadcasting information that is considered deviant by its very nature (Cohen 1972: 17-19). These stories serve as a warning, spurring an angry public to "formulate theories and plans, make speeches, write letters to the newspaper" (Ibid. 1972: 30) in anticipation of an inevitable events at some future time or continued occurrences (Ibid. 1972: 38) that have infiltrated society. Media sensationalism is therefore not only an effective means to transmit information that feeds moral panics, but also ensures their continuance by exaggerating the threat and maintaining its prominence in reporting.

RECOGNIZING AND DISTINGUISHING MORAL PANICS

The concept of moral panics has previously been associated with a variety of sociological studies, including drug abuse, juvenile delinquency, flag burning, AIDS, motorcycle gangs, and pedophilia (See Cohen 1972; Critcher 2003; Goode and Ben-Yehuda 1994; Hier 2002; Katz 2011; Morgan, Dagistanli, and Greg 2010; Welch 2000; Young 1971). Although several studies have explored the moral panics of terrorism (See Kappeler and Kappeler 2004; Rothe and Muzzatti 2004; Welch 2003), there have been additional moral panics against immigrants and non-citizens as a consequence of the societal conditions created by the "war on terror". As subjects of increased formal social control and negative informal social control, moral panics and the criminalization of immigrants and non-citizens may be discovered as noted through the consequences of defining, explaining, and labeling immigration as a social problem (Ward 2002: 466), as manifested in post 9/11 society's "war on terror".

Given that "social problems differ from moral panics in lacking folk devils, panicky reactions or wild fluctuations of concern" (Critcher 2003: 23), this analysis concentrates on "the socially significant differentiation of deviants from the non-deviant *population*...[which is] increasingly contingent upon circumstances of situation, place, social and personal biography, and the bureaucratically organized activities of agencies of social control" (Kitsuse 1962: 256). This investigation therefore observes the existence of heightened concern and labeling of immigrants and non-citizens as deviant or criminal, encouraged by both formal and informal social control mechanisms, prevalent since the September 11th attacks.

There was and may still be a moral panic against immigration in US society and therefore, the social consequences of "war on terror", have produced 1) an increase in suspicion and criminal labeling of immigrants and non-citizens; 2) changes in public opinion and support for immigration levels of non-US citizens; and 3) changes in the types and numbers of immigrants admitted into society, due to new processing and administration policies; thus contributing to a moral panic environment and the subsequent criminalization of immigration in U.S. society.

CHAPTER 2

September 11th and the War on Terror

Although historically terrorism has been a relatively rare occurrence in the United States, increasing attacks since the 1990s and the major attack in 2001 have propelled the issues of terrorism, national security, and immigration to the domestic forefront. The consequences of the September 11th attacks have therefore fundamentally changed the social organization of America. An examination of the moral panic conception as related to the changes in national security and immigration policy and support among the public, in the context of post 9/11 America, may reveal the lingering social consequences of the "war on terror" and impending social implications on U.S. society.

The post 9/11 social order consists of a complex chain of social interactions that include moral entrepreneurs and the media as "claims makers" (Hier 2002a: 313; McRobbie and Thornton 1995: 561) contributing to ideal conditions for moral panics. It is under these conditions that the PATRIOT Act, America's remedy for terrorism, has potentially aided in labeling immigrants and foreign visitors as threats, thus breaking from its regulatory social control foundation into moral panics. As one of the consequences of the PATRIOT Act and the subsequent implementation of new federal government regulations, U.S. society may have inadvertently begun to wage a subtle "war on immigrants".

Although not an overt expression in the media, among the public, or even at the federal level, moral panics may have erupted in American society and caused a sweeping distrust of immigrants (Chang 2002) and a suspicion of their motives in visiting and immigrating to the United States. Consequently, fear, suspicion, and distrust are directed against aliens, immigrants, and foreign visitors, at several levels of society. With a logical model and application of the of the moral panic conception, in the context of post-9/11 society, this analysis seeks to determine whether or not the U.S. is indeed presently immersed in moral panics, resulting in the subsequent criminalization of immigration.

SEPTEMBER 11th, 2001

For most Americans, the date September 11th, 2001 will be eternally remembered as "it was, in fact, one of those moments in which history splits, and we define the world as 'before' and 'after'" (*New York Times* 2001). The immediate and obvious response to the 9/11 strikes by the federal government was to label the attacks as foreign terrorism against the U.S. It then became clear that the Bush Administration resolved to treat the attacks as "acts of war by foreign aggressors" instead of seeking a solution and appropriate remedy under the jurisdiction of the criminal justice system (Whitehead and Aden 2002:1087), thus also turning the attention to immigrants and all types of foreign visitors. With the focus on immigrants and foreigners, the "war on terror" is a socially constructed problem, based on suspicion, rather than actual events or terrorist incidents that have historically occurred in the United States of America.

TERRORISM, THE UNITED STATES, AND THE "WAR ON TERROR"

The practice of terrorism, defined as "violence or threat of violence undertaken to create alarm and fear" (Klegley 2003: 1), is not a new phenomenon. In fact, terrorism is fundamentally miscellaneous, difficult to qualify, and highly subjective by definition (Rothe and Muzzatti 2004). Therefore, the recognition of terrorist acts and the consequences of terrorism may only be characterized by other historical acts that are defined as such. It may thus be presumed that:

> [P]robably the most significant contribution of sociological thinking to our understanding of terrorism is the realization that it is a social construction...terrorism is not a given in the real world but is instead an interpretation of events and their presumed causes. (Turk 2004: 271)

Even in contemporary American society, the Federal Bureau of Investigation (FBI) concurs that there is no singular or universal definition of terrorism. However, the agency formally defines terrorism as "the unlawful use of force and violence against persons or property to intimidate or coerce a government, the civilian population, or any segment thereof, in furtherance of political or social objectives" (FBI 2001). It was not until 1976 when then FBI director William Webster recognized and began to treat terrorism cases with a clearly defined strategy, even officially changing the title of particular types of investigations from "domestic security" to "terrorism" (Smith 1994: 8). Given the FBI's official recognition of terrorist acts, the current perception of terrorism and associated activities were thus established in 1980.

The 1980s began with a steadily increasing trend of terrorist incidents in the United States. This disturbing development resulted in the prompt escalation of the FBI's counter-terrorism efforts by 1982, with a renewed focus on identifying and concentrating on these types of crimes (Smith 1994). With the FBI's counter terrorism initiatives in place, the incidents peaked in 1983, with 51 attacks, and began a steady decline for the rest of the decade, ending with just 4 incidents in 1989 (Ibid: 18). The FBI eventually designated 219 crimes as official acts of terrorism that occurred in America between 1980 and 1989 (Ibid: 17). The bulk of the 1980s attacks were carried out by domestic terrorists, including religious, ethnic, right wing, leftist, and other special interest groups that used aggression and violence to affect social change (Ibid). However, by the 1990s the terrorist agenda began to change from political or social objectives, to those intent on "inflict[ing] massive and indiscriminant casualties within civilian populations" (FBI 2001: *Conclusion*).

The 1990s terrorist incidents were ushered in by several minor attacks in Puerto Rico followed by the February 1993 attack on the World Trade Center in New York. This attack marked the first modern international act of terrorism that was successfully carried out in America, killing 6 people and injuring over 1000 (FBI 2001: *Casualties of Terrorism 1980-2001*). Just two years later, the Oklahoma City bombing of the U.S. federal building in 1995, carried out by U.S. citizen Timothy McVeigh, injured 754 and killed 169 people; which was at that point, the largest number of deaths occurring due to a single act of terrorism in American history (Ibid). The new millennium began with most of the terrorist incidents carried out by domestic special interest groups, particularly extremist animal rights and environmental groups, again switching the focus and targeting equipment and facilities rather than individuals or groups of people. Then, returning the objective to the annihilation of civilian targets, the most prolific terrorist act committed on U.S. soil occurred on September 11th, 2001, injuring an estimated 12,000 and killing over 2,700 people, substantially exceeding the death toll of all other preceding acts of terrorism combined (Ibid: *Conclusion*).

With the increase in the frequency and lethality of terrorist incidents on U.S. soil in the 1990s, especially punctuated by the unprecedented attack on September 11th, the U.S. federal government was compelled to respond to terrorism with equal resolve. Through the interpretation of these terrorist acts and presumption of the causes, the U.S. government formulated their response to terrorism by constructing the "war on terror" that focuses its PATRIOT Act and subsequent legislation on increasing national security and includes several measures that enhance the social control of immigrants and non-citizens. Although its primary intention is to increase anti-terrorism efforts, the PATRIOT Act has also effectively laid out the Bush Administration's intentions with a decidedly negative wariness of immigrants and foreign visitors in America.

As the Act is drafted, some of the specific clauses enable the U.S. government to target immigrants, critically reducing rights, freedoms, and liberties and inadvertently criminalizing their presence in the country. Beginning with the implementation of the Act, the federal government's reaction has in fact illuminated "the state's ability to label people as terrorists or terrorist sympathizers, no matter how absurd or far-fetched, works to position those so labeled as non-citizens, outside the moral community, to whom human rights bear no relevance" (McCulloch 2002: 57). It is therefore, the reaction of the federal government, in addition to the intended fear terrorism has created, that has promoted moral panics against immigration and foreign visitors in the United States.

THE USA PATRIOT ACT OF 2001

On September 20th, 2001 in an address to a joint session of Congress and the American people, President Bush requested that all other nations commit to the U.S. fight against terrorism declaring, "either you are with us, or you are with the terrorists" (Bush 2001). Before that time, U.S. counterterrorism efforts were "composed of a series of loosely aligned agencies which had disparate policies and shared little information...with counter-terrorism responsibilities dispersed among some 100 governmental agencies" (Shutt and Deflem, 2005). With more of a reactive strategy for responding to terrorist acts and given the covert planning and execution of the September 11th attacks, both detection and proactive prevention were severely encumbered. It was under these conditions that it may have been difficult, if not impossible to forecast, prepare for, or respond to such a devastating attack, since within the federal administration, fighting international terrorism did not even have a clearly defined strategy (Duffy 2003).

Within one week of the strikes, U.S. authorities determined that "16 of the 19 suspected hijackers who commandeered American jetliners entered the United States with legal visas" (Slevin and Sheridan 2001: A06); instantly casting doubt on the effectiveness of and safety measures imposed by the U.S. immigration system with regard to aliens entering the country. In addition to the attention paid to foreigners, even the name of the Act is one of the "most clever and symbolically powerful Washington acronyms of all time. It not only found the right words to spell out the title for the act, but it wrapped the legislation in the cloak of patriotism" (Kettl 2004: 96), further implicating aliens, immigrants, and foreign born citizens as outsiders and potential threats and in effect, branding them as explicit targets in the "war on terror".

In order to fight the "war on terror" in post-September 11th society, the United States Congress passed a series of new federal legislative initiatives, collectively hailed as the PATRIOT Act. The Act was approved almost unanimously by the Senate, in a vote of 98 in favor and only 1 dissenting, and by a substantial margin in the House, 357 in support with just 66 in opposition (*United States Department of Justice* 2001). The Act is, "exceedingly long and complex, comprising ten-parts and over 300 pages" (Whitehead and Aden 2002: 1088) which covers "350 subject areas, encompassing 40 federal agencies and carrying 21 legal amendments" (Thomas 2002: 94), designed as a means to combat terrorism, primarily through an extensive increase in border protection, intelligence gathering, and law enforcement expenditures. The PATRIOT Act also grants the federal government broad surveillance capabilities and increased social control mechanisms to further strengthen terrorism prevention efforts, in the name of national security.

The PATRIOT Act and subsequent legislation specifically related to the "war on terror" have been largely controversial because these initiatives institute the most significant social changes or consequences as anti-terrorist measures, effecting both citizens and non-citizens. The Act includes measures that test the limits of the several Constitutional Amendments, including freedom of speech, due process, protection from search and seizures, and privacy protections (Chang 2002). Many challengers suggest that the PATRIOT Act's increased power in the area of surveillance most interferes with citizens' rights to privacy under the Fourth Amendment (Whitehead 2002). The measure allows warrantless wiretapping and access to personal records such as medical, financial, business, educational, library, and electronic or computer tracking of both citizens and non-citizens (Thomas 2002: 96). Thus, these changes in legislation pose significant dangers to the violation of inherent rights and freedoms granted to U.S. citizens (Martin 2004) while stripping virtually all Constitutional rights previously afforded to lawful resident aliens (Parenti 2002).

In addition to better access to personal records, law enforcement is granted the ability to subpoena third party records from telephone companies and Internet service providers in order to strengthen surveillance powers (Chang 2002). The result causes an erosion of "the line between intelligence gathering and gathering evidence for criminal proceedings. It expands the ability of government to spy by wiretaps and computer surveillance. It provides access to medical, financial, business and educational records and allows secret searches of homes and offices" (Thomas 2002: 96). There are also so called "sneak-and-peak searches", now included in all criminal investigations, not just terrorism-related investigations, are permissible as covert home or office searches that do not require notice until after the search has been conducted (Chang 2002). Although these measures apply to all U.S. residents, there are also various clauses in the PATRIOT Act that apply specifically to immigrants and non-citizens.

The PATRIOT Act includes a number of miscellaneous provisions that enhance the federal government's ability to "deny entry to, detain, prosecute, and remove foreign nationals suspected of being involved in terrorist activities" (Lebowitz and Podheiser 2002: 876). Of these provisions, Section 412 of the PATRIOT Act is often cited as perhaps the most controversial immigration-related measure; a provision allowing non-citizens suspected of terrorist activity to be subjected to mandatory and indefinite detention and deportation, "irrespective of any relief from deportation that they may be eligible for or granted" (Ibid: 879). Further, new detention measures allow the Attorney General to broadly define and certify what is a terrorist organization and thus order the detainment of even a "lawful permanent resident, simply by certifying that he has 'reasonable grounds to believe' that the individual 'is described in' the immigration law's antiterrorism provisions" (Cole 2004: 1776). Opponents frequently argue that methods outlined in the PATRIOT Act that enable the defining, certifying, and detaining of aliens are shrouded in secrecy (Cole 2002; Lyon 2003; Welch 2003) and are an absolute violation of due process (Chang 2002; Smith 2005; Whitehead 2002). So far, these measures have been relatively unsuccessful in that:

As of January 2004, the government had detained more than 5000 foreign nationals through its antiterrorist efforts...None of these detainees had been determined to be involved with al Qaeda or the September 11th conspiracy...[except one] lone conviction – for conspiring to support some unspecified terrorist activity in the unspecified future. (Cole 2004: 1753-1754)

These types of broadly defined anti-terrorism measures that garner the most attention from opponents and "greatly [concern] civil libertarians and immigrants' rights groups, particularly in light of racial profiling and scapegoating, mass detentions and mistreatment, and the government's refusal to disclose information about those detained" (Welch 2002: 188). Although detainment and deportation have gained much of the media attention, there are additional measures subsequent to the PATRIOT Act that also restrict and affect the daily lives of legal aliens in a variety of new ways.

Since the implementation of the PATRIOT Act in 2001, several federal initiatives have been enacted to improve the tracking and control of aliens and non-citizens. By 2004, the federal government implemented new measures that impose additional scrutiny upon aliens that are legally admitted into the country, for purpose of preserving national security. Examples of these tracking systems include: voluntary and special registration of non-citizens from particular countries that are suspected of having connections to terrorist organizations, with the ultimate objective of registering all foreign nationals; restricted driver's licensing requirements that vary by state, usually requiring several forms of documentation to prove lawful residence and limiting the validation length to visa or lawful residency end dates; mandatory student enrollment in the Student and Exchange Visitor Information System (SEVIS), that monitors foreign students' movements and academic progress; and the United States Visitor and Immigrant Status Indicator Technology (US-VISIT), a biometric information system effectively that tracks foreign nationals entering the U.S. until they exit the country (Nguyen 2005).

Overall, the 9/11 reactionary measures, collectively assigned to fight the "war on terror", have caused an abrupt and considerable modification in the way the U.S. handles issues of immigration. Even with a relatively flexible and interminable history of immigration, the challenges arising from the "war on terror" since September 11th have materialized as "America went from being a nation of immigrants to a nation of suspects" (McKenzie 2004: 1149).

FEDERAL IMMIGRATION POLICY

Considerably exceeding any other nation in the last two centuries, the United States has admitted more immigrants into the country, in varying degrees, based on a diverse set of socioeconomic and foreign policy considerations (Meyers 2004). America's immigration system has therefore remained both fluid and accommodating to aliens, foreign visitors, and immigrants alike. In fact, immigration in the U.S. has moved through an array of stages, from virtually no restrictions on the number and types of people immigrating until the 1920s to a national origin quota system (Isbister 1996). More recently, federal controls have readjusted the immigration strategy to decrease the family-sponsored backlog and accommodate more highly skilled workers, increasing per country limits and expanding work-based categories of immigrants admitted (Clark 2003: 54-55). Even though immigration is numerically restricted by predetermined per country limits, there are a variety of issues and concerns that further alter the number and kinds of immigrants admitted into the country each year.

Annual immigration mirrors the existing federal regime's political and ideological ambitions and includes a variety of other issues that have great influence on legislative, legal, and policy implementations. Historically, "policy on permanent immigration was shaped by the state of the economy, large-scale immigration of dissimilar composition, wars, foreign policy considerations, and liberal/racist ideological trends" (Meyers 2004: 27). Although the PATRIOT Act was not drafted as an immigration policy, its main focus is immigration with much of the new legislation and changes in strategy attributed to increased national security concerns, designed to reduce and deter foreign terrorists from attempting to gain entry into the country and to enhance the control over legal aliens in the country.

With increased security checks, features, and restrictions, policies therefore have a tendency to reflect a negative view of aliens, illegal and legal, since the attacks of September 11th. In fact, the majority of the PATRIOT Act measures provide immigration control enhancements that both restrict legal immigration and revitalize and renew federal concerns that began in the late 1980s with regard to illegal or undocumented immigrants.

Illegal Immigration and the Undocumented

Although enforcing illegal immigration has always been an obstinate issue for the federal government, it was not until 1986 when the Immigration Reform and Control Act (IRCA) was implemented as the "first U.S. immigration law specifically targeted toward the undocumented" (Hayes 2001:4). The IRCA, characterized as an amnesty program, was designed and enacted as means to reduce the backlog of family-sponsored applicants, give legal status to the undocumented already residing in the U.S., and diminish the entry of illegal or undocumented immigrants (Clark 2003: 54), arriving mostly through the porous Mexican border as migrant laborers. Although the strategy was directed at decreasing the number of illegal immigrants, the practical policy on immigration continued to be "influenced by the economic factors...and to a lesser extent by other factors" (Meyers 2004: 27), thus continuing and encouraging lenience to the large volume of willing, undocumented workers entering the country.

Essentially, even as the new 1986 laws were implemented, many service and agriculture sectors came to depend on the undocumented as a form of reliable, cheap labor that aids in keeping production costs down while contributing to the growth of the economy (Bischoff 2002: 269-270). The IRCA therefore had little impact on the existing illegal presence as economic conditions continued to sustain the steady flow of undocumented immigrants to the United States. Real changes and restrictions to immigration policies were not effectively realized until the passage of new federal immigration measures in the beginning in the 1990s.

Designed primarily as mechanisms to control the illegal immigration flow, the Immigration Act of 1990 and the Illegal Immigration Reform and Immigrant Responsibility Act of 1996 (IIRIRA) increased the per-country limits, number of visas issued, and funding for border control and illegal immigrant apprehension efforts (Clark 2003: 54). Additionally, new policies lessening the benefits extended to immigrants, in the form of welfare and public services, were imposed with the Personal Responsibility and Work Opportunity Reconciliation Act of 1996 (Ibid: 54).

The 1996 laws marked the last series of major changes to the U.S. federal immigration policy, which greatly affected the rights and privileges afforded to both illegal and legal immigrants entering the U.S. and the number and types of immigrants admitted, until September 11th, 2001. Since then, most of the problems and attention given to federal immigration policy occurs with respect to illegal immigration and controlling the flow of the undocumented. However, the image ascribed to immigrants beginning in the 1990s and in much of the new legislation since October 2001, has reinforced negative social concerns directed towards immigration and all types of aliens present in U.S. society.

Blurring Lines Between Legal and Illegal Immigration

Changes to the 1990s immigration laws focused on illegal immigration. However, legal immigrants also felt the impact as "legislation on immigration in 1996 was imbued with an undifferentiated fear of crime, outsiders, and minorities" (Welch 2002: 66) implicating not just the undocumented, but stereotyping all immigrants as potential deviants, threats, or a source of social problems in U.S. society. These types of laws contribute to the construction of immigration as a social problem as:

> [T]here is often a slippage between the categories of illegal immigrant and legal immigrant. Both get constructed as 'other' to those who naturally belong and become associated with a host of social dangers and disorders such as crime, drug trafficking, and terrorism. (Doty 2003: 41)

Since the terrorist attacks of 9/11, the separation between legal and illegal immigrants has blurred even further. This may be due in part to the focus of the PATRIOT Act on national security and border protection; in which increased prevention efforts against illegal entry and control over legal admission are of paramount concern and garner equal attention.

Ultimately, the creation and enforcement of laws designed to fight the "war on terror" have exposed a host of complex and divisive social concerns relating to immigration. A harmful impact is particularly noted with regard to lawful immigrants since,

> [I]n reality legal and illegal immigration cannot so unproblematically be separated. This is especially the case when it comes to immigrants' rights. Efforts to deal with illegal immigration often have significant effects on those immigrants who are here legally. (Doty 2003: 33)

This is most evident with post-9/11 national security controls and tracking systems that are designed to detect terrorist threats and illegal aliens, but negatively impact immigrants with legal status.

As new policies relating to immigration continue to be implemented, legal aliens are gradually becoming more subjected to tracking systems and surveillance controls. With these types controls pertaining to all entrants, foreign nationals entering the U.S. are immediately placed into a tracking system and therefore labeled as potential suspects, criminals, or threats to society. Accordingly, regarding all aliens as potential threats inadvertently implies the image of *folk devils*, thus creating an ideal environment where a moral panic may indeed occur against all types of immigrants and foreign visitors entering the country.

THE MORAL PANIC ENVIRONMENT

Since the terrorist attacks on September 11th and the subsequent implementation of the PATRIOT Act, it may be apparent that the effects of the "war on terror" on the American psyche, changes to immigration laws, and the blurring of legal and illegal categories have created an ideal moral panic environment against immigration. The panicked environment is not arbitrary but instead is manifested as social concerns that intensify and escalate into panics against identifiable social threats, labeled as *folk devils*, under particular conditions. Cohen (1972) distinguishes the panic environment as:

> A condition, episode, person or group of persons [that] emerges to become defined as a threat to societal values and interests; its nature is presented in a stylized and stereotypical fashion by the mass media...at other times it has more serious and long-lasting repercussions and might produce such changes as those in legal and social policy. (p. 9)

Given this scenario, once a threat to society or "folk devil" is determined, three additional distinct participant groups further contribute to the creation of moral panic conditions: the government, the public, and the media.

PANIC PARTICIPANTS

The Government and Formal Social Controls.

A shift towards increased formal means of social control is especially evident after social norms have been amended, following a momentous society-changing event (Crawford 2004; Newman 2003). Similarly, during a moral panic episode the government addresses social concerns over salient societal threats or *folk devils* by inducing and/or enhancing social controls. As formal social control mechanisms become more evident:

> Perhaps the most important interface in the control culture is that where state control in the form of legislation and legislators meets pressures of public opinion as channeled by claims-makers and moral entrepreneurs. This is particularly important where the

moral entrepreneurs are themselves politicians. (Thompson 1998: 37-38)

As moral entrepreneurs, the Bush Administration's response to the 9/11 attacks first concentrated on increasing formal controls by creating the Department of Homeland Security (DHS); a single federal entity that enveloped 22 existing agencies and united all the divisions responsible for each aspect of national security, including immigration services. In merging these segments, the intention was to "take a more focused and streamlined approach to homeland defense, combining the skills and responsibilities of nearly two dozen federal agencies" (Timms 2004: 37), that the public could rely on to determine risk levels, balance freedom with security, and ultimately provide protection from threats to U.S. society (Kettl 2004). Several weeks later, the addition of formal social controls continued as the federal government increased its capacity to manage society and enhance security through the passage of anti-terrorist legislation in the form of the PATRIOT Act (Cole 2004; Collins 2002; Whitehead and Aden 2002).

Although most obvious since September 11ᵗʰ are the creation of the DHS and the enactment of new federal legislation, society's moral entrepreneurs use a variety of supplementary claims making means to both generate and sustain support for the terrorism agenda; an endeavor that is especially apparent in a moral panic environment. Some examples of claims making activities that occur during a panic episode include:

Attempting to influence public opinion by discussing the supposed extent of the threat in the media; forming organizations and even generating entire social movements to deal with the problems the threat presumably poses; giving talks or conducting seminars to inform the public how to counter the threat in question; attempting to get certain views approved in educational curricula; influencing legislators to allocate funds which would deal with a given threat; discrediting spokespersons who advocate alternative, opposing, or competing perspectives. (Goode and Ben-Yehuda 1994: 82)

In fact, since the "war on terror" began, the federal government has used numerous panic inducing methods, most commonly invoked by claims makers in the construction and continuance of presumed social problems relating to the "war on terror".

In the post-9/11 social environment, claims making is frequently summoned as a means to aid in the construction and maintenance of the "war on terror", by keeping relevant social concerns such as immigration and national security in the domestic spotlight. Additionally, formal social controls accommodate, "objectives [that] seem to maintain public fear by repeated warnings of attack, to keep terrorism at the forefront of our imaginations" (Berry 2004: 160), and ultimately to uphold continued support from other panic participants; namely the media and the public.

The Mass Media and the Public

Through continuously available reports from television, Internet, and printed media, the public's understanding of cultural issues relies heavily on the news as a means of updating, interpreting, and formulating perceptions of current events. This ubiquitous accessibility enables the media to have "five effects on public opinion: they stabilize prevailing opinions, set priorities, elevate events and issues, sometimes change opinions, and ultimately limit options" (Paletz and Entman 1981:189). Given its fundamental role in conveying information to the public, the mass media therefore serves as the principal instrument in influencing the public's collective beliefs and cultivating post-September 11th social conditions.

In a claims-making role, formal social control mechanisms, such as the government, are a favorable partner for the media as they "seize on topics presented within the problem frame to help propel their causes" (Altheide 2002:142). Moreover, with the assistance of formal social controls:

> We should realize that the press is not just a stenographer for power, faithfully echoing what authorities feed it. It plays a far more proactive role as propagandist for the ruling ideology, exercising its own initiative to soften up public opinion, telling people what to think about events even before the events have played out, clearing the way for policymakers to make their moves. (Parenti 2002: 9)

In conjunction with the government, the media therefore set post-9/11 social conditions by aiding in determining, evaluating, and promoting social concerns relating to terrorism, while providing daily coverage of events that convey the government's commitment to the "war on terror".

Likewise, moral panics are fueled by formal social controls, supported by enacted laws and increased control mechanisms, and embellishment by aggressive media reporting techniques, thus justifying any consequent moral outcry among the public (Cohen 1972; Goode and Ben-Yehuda 1994). In any social environment, a moral outcry or social concern directed against a particular individual or group may occur as:

> *[S]ocial groups create deviance by making the rules whose infraction constitutes deviance,* and by applying those rules to particular people and labeling them as outsiders... they cannot assume that these people have actually committed a deviant act or broken some rule, because the process of labeling may not be infallible; some people may be labeled deviant who in fact have not broken a rule. (Becker 1963: 9; italics in original)

The combined efforts of the government and mass media therefore aid the public in collectively confirming and identifying alleged social problems or concerns. Basically, these groups, even if unsubstantiated, are commonly manifested and subsequently labeled as "outsiders" or identifiable individuals or groups that deviate from social norms.

The way that deviance or criminality may be defined as a social problem comes from "social interactions between ordinary people, journalists, and sources of information within the structural and political-economic context of active processes of news construction and crime management" (Barak 1994: 6); resulting in a general or collectively held belief. In essence, the media and formal social controls respond to the alleged social problems that are correspondingly created when a substantial number of members of a given society have a common concern that is regarded as a problem. Once recognized, the problem necessitates some form of official action to correct the situation (Goode and Ben-Yehuda 1994).

Especially true since the 1990s immigration legislation and throughout the post-9/11 era, media frequently broadcasts claims by both political rhetoric and law enforcement officials that enhance the impression that "terrorism has found a place in the public explanation for crime-reinforcing other previously constructed social problems" (Kappeler and Kappeler 2004: 188). Moreover, in a moral panic environment, it is the media in partnership with society's moral entrepreneurs that "neither reflect nor create public opinion; they construct it" (Critcher 2003: 138).

A "Culture of Fear": Amplifying Deviance

In the social control role, the PATRIOT Act's increased cost of counter-terrorism measures to society combined with the widening of responsibility of government and law enforcement agencies has created a new "culture of fear" in the United States. A "culture of fear" is fostered as "a single anomalous event can provide us with multiple groups of people to fear" (Glassner 1999: xiii). In that capacity, the post-9/11 media has been paramount as "policing issues and events take on greater significance as we are exposed to more messages and images about reasons or threats to safety and as life is viewed more risky, dangerous, and fearful" (Altheide 2002: 134). Essentially, with the ability to provide continuous reporting, the "war on terror" and its sponsors furnish the media with constant updates and enable terrorism, immigration, and national security to remain the top social concerns, necessitating daily deliberation and interpretation directed toward the general public.

At varying times in history, particular groups of people have been demonized by the public, typically with the assistance of mass media and the support of the federal government, aiding to spread enthusiasm (Bonn 2011; Cohen 1972; Goode and Ben-Yehuda 1994; McRobbie and Thornton 1995). Beginning with Cohen's (1972) study of the social construction of heightened concern over Mods and Rockers, these episodes are characterized as moral panics and serve to explain the spread of hysteria and the creation of social controls and public attitudes, ultimately discernible as social concerns or problems. In the post-9/11 social environment, the "war on terror" may have created ideal conditions for a moral panic on immigration as:

> Perhaps the most prominent fear, on the topic at hand, is fear of an unknown and unpredictable terrorist attack. There are also fears of being accused of being unpatriotic, thus creating fear of reprisals from one's own people. But fear of 'the other,' the outsider-terrorist, seems to be taking precedence in the U.S. presently. (Berry 2004: 161)

In addition to identifying the potential panic participants and possible *folk devils*, an exploration of the essential social conditions that exist during a moral panic is also critical and can provide a calculable assessment.

MEASURING THE PANIC: INDICATORS OF MORAL PANICS

Moral panics should not be confused with other social problems or issues that demand the public's attention during a crisis period. There are in fact, very specific conditions that must be present in order to formally define a moral panic environment. In order to more decisively establish the presence of moral panics in society, Goode and Ben-Yehuda (1994) proposed at least five requisite elements or criteria that precisely outline and characterize a moral panic environment: concern, hostility, consensus, disproportionality, and volatility.

Concern

The concern indicator is characterized as the general development of heightened anxiety over the behavior of a particular group or groups of people that is measurable and may be most evident through the media, public opinion polls, proposed legislation, and among the general public (Goode and Ben-Yehuda 1994). Critcher (2003) suggested three questions that must be considered in any attempt to establish the indicator of concern in a moral panic environment: "who becomes concerned about this issue?; how widespread is this concern?; and how is it expressed?" (p. 29). As evidenced in previous moral panic incidents, such as the "war on drugs", the concern indicator is most suitably assessed by observing changes in poll data and media attention given to particular social issues.

During the latter half of the 1980s, the U.S. was immersed in a moral panic as "drug use, abuse, and misuse emerged into the limelight as perhaps never before" (Goode and Ben-Yehuda 1994: 203). Beginning with the Reagan Administration in the early 1980s, America began to wage a "war on drugs" that continued throughout the decade and peaked in 1989 with the establishment of the Office of National Drug Control Policy, the executive branch charged with carrying out the president's drug enforcement agenda (Bertram et al. 1996). In its familiar claims making role, the federal government routinely addressed the public with unprecedented and ever widening authority, broadcasting and publicizing the social ills and damaging effects of drugs on society.

As one of the many consequences of moral panics, laws or formal social control mechanisms as related to drug policy and enforcement were greatly affected in the 1980s "war on drugs". Essentially, lawmakers and politicians as claims makers ardently advocated robust legislative changes thus increasing their power to control and regulate the social system (Welch 2000: 110), in order to appropriately address rising social concerns. In fact, during the 1980s, "government support for extraordinary measures was paralleled by a public willingness to sacrifice fundamental democratic freedoms in pursuit of the drug war" (Bertram et al. 1996: 116). As evidenced by those polled, as many as 62% actually indicated a willingness to give up several rights and freedoms in order to aid in the "war on drugs" and the majority indicated a willingness to subscribe to home searches and warrantless searches (Ibid: 116).

Essentially, because of the threat that drug users posed on society, the majority of Americans were willing to take an active role in the "war on drugs" by surrendering some of their inherent rights and freedoms for the cause. Given the overall concern that developed in society because of the drug war, moral panics then became even more obvious as hostility toward a targeted group intensified.

Hostility

Hostility in moral panics is exemplified as disdain for a responsible party or group that is collectively labeled as the enemy, deviant, or criminal and is seen as posing a threat to the rest of society (Goode and Ben-Yehuda 1994). Oftentimes, claims makers designate a group that is considered as the enemy, thus evoking a struggle between good and evil, where a division is made between the decent majority and a clearly delineated deviant segment, stereotyped as *folk devils* (Cohen 1972; Goode and Ben-Yehuda 1994). The act of stereotyping also allows the general public to place the *folk devil* in a "despised category... [which] permits the conventional member of a society to feel justified in strong, even savage condemnation... unambiguous hostility toward him or her should not only be expected – it is demanded" (Ibid: 72). The hostility indicator may therefore be determined by establishing a defined enemy and the declaration of the threat they pose to a given society, and clearly demarcating a *folk devil* (Critcher 2003: 29).

As with the concern indicator in moral panics, hostility may be determined though observing the measured increase of both formal and informal social controls as related to the declared *folk devils*. In the "war on drugs", President Bush named *folk devils* in broad terms, declaring that Americans should "'face this evil as a nation united... victory over drugs is our cause, a just cause" (Bertram et al. 1996: 114). During the drug war, federal administration representatives and various agency officials frequently displayed their hostility publicly, declaring that there was "nothing 'morally' wrong with beheading drug traffickers"; "casual drug users 'ought to be taken out and shot'"; "the death penalty should be used against large-scale dealers"; and "planes that were even suspected of carrying drugs should be shot down" (Ibid: 115-116). It was these types of statements that fuelled the president's harsh anti-drug tactics, convinced the general public of the danger that drugs posed to society, and ultimately justified the "war on drugs" and any resultant enactment of laws, loss of civil liberties, and increased funding that occurred.

Among the public, new drug war policies virtually erased all lines between the previous drug abuse classifications, including the more socially acceptable casual user and the other more serious type of addict, indicating that the "war on drugs" approach had zero tolerance, favoring the fervent pursuit of all drug users (Bertram et al. 1996: 116). Once the foundation was in place, it was just a matter of time before the public joined the drug war, again displaying their support for tough new laws, willingness to be subjected to testing, even at the expense of personal privacy and increased taxation, and general contempt for drug users, indicated by strong support for harsher sentencing and more severe punishments (Clymer 1986). A generalized concern and hostile sentiment toward *folk devils* in society may therefore be complemented by ever increasing anxiety that manifests as consensus in the moral panic environment.

Consensus

Once concern and hostility are evident, consensus is reached when there is widespread agreement that a particular action or behavior is considered injurious to a whole society and it is agreed that there is a real threat, caused by a clearly defined responsible group or party (Goode and Ben-Yehuda 1994). Although there is some combined overlap in the notion of consensus, from the concern and hostility indicators, this indicator differs in that there is the addition of a looming or ominous significance in the source of the threat that requires an organized resistance to its presence (Critcher 2003: 29).

The level of consensus over drug abuse among the general public eventually reached its highest level of recognition as evidenced by poll data that indicated pollsters named the number one domestic problem in America as drug abuse, going from just 2% in 1986 (Goode and Ben-Yehuda 1994), up to 20% by July 1989 (Bertram et al. 1996) then just two months later, soaring to 64% in September 1989 (Bertram et al. 1996; Goode and Ben-Yehuda 1994). The increase has been attributed to the federal government's public promotion of its focused agenda on vastly improving drug laws and enforcement efforts, which were significantly aided by a sudden media blitz on the issue of drugs in America. It may also be noted that the media's prompt support coincided with a major presidential speech on the subject, suggesting, "anything goes" in the fight against the "war on drugs" (Bertram et al. 1996). Again, these types of increases in consensus of drug abuse among the public indicate that the successful, widespread construction of a social problem by claims makers, forced the majority of the public to be concerned and acquire some hostility so they were compelled to commit themselves to the "war on drugs".

Disproportionality

The disproportionality indicator is one of the most difficult aspects to quantify and ultimately ascertain in moral panics. In fact, conclusive determinations and certainty become elusive goals in the moral panic environment as disproportionality is assessed by "the *implication* that public concern is *in excess* of *what is appropriate if concern were directly proportional* to objective harm (Goode and Ben-Yehuda 1994: 36; emphasis added). Nevertheless, Goode and Ben-Yehuda (1994) further assert that disproportionality must be empirical in nature and can be clarified by additional requirements, which include exaggerated and/or fabricated figures, other harmful conditions, and changes in the concern over time.

In order to promote a claim or increase public awareness about a supposed social problem claims makers and moral entrepreneurs may increase the frequency of reports, inflate, or fabricate figures used to depict a social concern (Goode and Ben-Yehuda 1994). Orcutt and Turner (1993) examined 1980s reporting on drug abuse, finding that the extent of the drug crisis among high school students was vastly distorted by due to the manipulation of statistics and graphical accounts by the media. The use of abbreviated and rescaled axes in *Newsweek, The New York Times,* and other popular printed media reporting, gave the illusion of intensified yearly changes in usage, thus adding "conceptual energy to the ominous image of a growing epidemic" (Orcutt and Turner 1993: 203). Even with, "objective data that indicated no significant increases in the consumption of illicit drugs" (Jensen, Gerber, and Babcock 1991: ¶38), the number of articles published on the subject of drug use/abuse reached record numbers in 1980s, peaking in 1986 (Ibid).

By and large, the unwarranted and exaggerated concern over drugs use among teens is an example of the federal government's widely publicized efforts to fight the "war on drugs" coupled with a record number of media reports on illicit drug use and abuse in the 1980s. Interestingly, Goode and Ben-Yehuda (1994) note that although illegal drugs typically generate a higher level of public concern and media attention, legal drugs such as tobacco and alcohol have proven to be equally if not more dangerous and disease causing (p. 44).

Volatility

As the final indicator of moral panics, volatility is denoted by the sudden eruption followed by a similarly abrupt dissipation of the episode (Goode and Ben-Yehuda 1994). Volatility tends to be cyclical in nature, perhaps remaining dormant for a period of time then rapidly re-emerging on occasion as sporadic incidents materialize (Ibid; Critcher 2003; Thompson 1998). The extent of a panic relies heavily on claims makers and media as "a 'new' social problem will be seized upon, covered until its full news potential has been exploited, then dropped as the next new problem, with its fresh new angles, is discovered" (Critcher 2003: 139).

Given its sudden development and abrupt decline, the volatility indicator was clearly discernible during the "war on drugs" panic in the 1980s. Reaching its peak in of 64% in the September 1989 public opinion polls, concern over drugs dropped to 38% by November, then steadily declined over the next year to 10%, and remained between 8 to 12% into the 1990s (Goode and Ben-Yehuda 1994: 207). Goode and Ben-Yehuda (1994) suggest that this type of the abrupt dissolution of a panic may be attributed to reduction in media reporting and general interest in particular issues, since among the public, "there is something of a 'carrying capacity' or saturation point of public attention " (p. 207). It follows that as public concern over particular social issues recesses; the coverage of the concern retracts into a dormant phase or disappears from governmental rhetoric and the media spotlight altogether.

Once the reasonably short cycle of a moral panic ends, the result is typically a return to similar social conditions that were present before the panic erupted, much like any fashion, fad, or craze (Goode and Ben-Yehuda 1994) that appears in many segments of society. Volatility is therefore dependent on collective beliefs or behavior in that the public takes an interest in a problem and just as quickly loses their enthusiasm as the related issues:

> [M]ay become *routinized* or *institutionalized*...moral concern about the target behavior results in, or remains in place in the form of, social movements, legislation, enforcement practices, informal interpersonal norms or practices for punishing transgressors, after it has run its course. (Goode and Ben-Yehuda 1994: 38-39)

Thus, once social concerns become institutionalized, many of the short and long-term changes to the social climate are observed, through "reactionary measures and punitive strategies...special hearings or sub-committees...zero tolerance policies...[and] tougher laws and harsher sentences" (Rothe and Muzzatti 2004: 329-330). Essentially, although moral panic episodes may be relatively short lived, there exists the potential for lasting social effects as "a litany of repressive social control strategies and mechanisms may be left in its wake" (Ibid: 330).

THE USA PATRIOT ACT OF 2001: SOCIAL CONTROL OF TERRORISM

With "enhanced powers to detain noncitizens, wiretap cell phones, intercept E-mails, and monitor Internet usage" (White 2004: 38), and drafted as: "an act to deter and punish terrorist acts in the United States and around the world, to enhance law enforcement investigatory tools, and for other purposes" (*United States Department of Justice* 2001), the PATRIOT Act provides a variety of concessions for broad federal powers of social control. Essentially, the implementation of the Act, has aided in establishing a "heightened sense of risk consciousness [that demonstrates}...how socially constructed problems are discursively transformed into a set of risks and dangers which serve political- and morally regulative -ends" (Hier 2002b: 36). Although not overt coercion, the ability and commitment of moral entrepreneurs to influence and effect change in society through the PATRIOT Act's social control mechanisms, is crucial in leading the citizenry to accept enhanced national security as means of institutionalization.

Additionally, as U.S. society has, through formal social controls, become more aware of the threats posed by modern terrorism, informal social controls have made citizens' understanding and opinions on various social issues, such as terrorism, national security, and immigration, more susceptible to influence; perhaps even increasing their suspicion towards particular groups or individuals living within society. With the continuation of perceived threats and potential for further harm, collective beliefs are thus established and developed, eventually governing societies through a combination of informal social controls and institutionalization; that is achieved through formal means. Given its focus on terrorism, the establishment of the PATRIOT Act has therefore adeptly employed both formal and informal social control mechanisms, to not only concentrate on issues related to national security and fighting the "war on terror", but also to other contingent social concerns such as immigration. It may therefore be evident that once enacted, the PATRIOT Act evolved from its formal social control roots and fostered an ideal environment for moral panics against immigration.

The Shift from Social Control to Moral Panics

With the introduction of any new federal laws or regulations, citizens are compelled to accept formal social control mechanisms as routine, allowing necessary changes where:

> [I]nstitutionalization occurs [as] new knowledge or beliefs become part of the organizations' bureaucratic routines: when processes that facilitate or constitute the

performance of the new belief are built into organizations' standard operating procedures and regulations. (Crawford 2004: 700)

Given the impact of the September 11th attacks, moral entrepreneurs predictably led in the creation of formal laws as "social control agents correspond to the organizations responsible in the rescue and remedy phases for dealing with the consequences of disaster" (Cohen 1972: 85). At the same time, the mass media and informal controls became part of the recovery from the 9/11 attacks in a supportive role, further publicizing and upholding the commitment of society's moral entrepreneurs to the "war or terror".

In the wake of the 9/11 terrorist attacks, the successful implementation and institutionalization of the PATRIOT Act is essential as the U.S. government cannot fight the "war on terror" alone. Rather, it is "a campaign that will require strong and sustained partnerships among the nation's federal, state, and local governments, between government and the private sector, and between the United States and the world community" (Kettl 2004: 127). Therefore, considering the vast communal and international concentration, aimed at the preservation of national security, measuring the effects of the "war on terror", the PATRIOT Act, and subsequent social control mechanisms on U.S. society may be most aptly assessed using the moral panic conception.

During a moral panic episode, individuals are led by their social perception, as an increased influence from society's formal and informal mechanisms of social control, determine their perceptions of social issues and subsequent levels of institutionalization. It is at this point that the federal government's means of social control may shift, manifesting as "the spiral effect produced by the interaction of the media, public opinion, interest groups and the authorities... [giving] rise to the phenomenon which has become known as a moral panic" (Thompson 1998: 7). Under these conditions the PATRIOT Act and subsequent federal regulations designed to fight the "war on terror" may be observed as moral panics against immigration in U.S. society.

In the initial stages of a moral panic, formal regulations are especially apparent as both concern and hostility toward a particular group of people conspicuously increases, ultimately identifying the group as a threat in a given society (Hawdon 2001; Thompson 1998). It is at this point in time when the perceived enemy or "folk devil functions to:

> [P]rovide a rallying point, a point upon which to focus hatred and rally in "defense" against. The construction of enemies gives us a dividing line between 'us' and 'them', with 'them' determined to be inferior and deserving of unequal treatment. (Berry 2004: 165)

Criminalization of Immigrants

With regard to immigrants in the post-9/11 era, enhanced formal and informal social controls may have produced a "folk devil" as, "the additional authority granted by the Patriot Act raises the very real specter of 'blacklisting' as an accepted immigration policy, reminiscent of McCarthyism in the 1950s" (Whitehead and Aden 2002: 1099). Although most immigrants strive to integrate into their new society, some of the post-September 11ᵗʰ regulations of the PATRIOT Act hinder them from gaining full acceptance. In addition to the tracking systems and new security visitor entry screenings at U.S. borders, immigrants are faced with a variety of obstacles even when attempting to acquire basic needs, such as driver's licenses, mortgage home loans, bank accounts, and many basic government benefits (Nguyen 2005). It is these types of social control mechanisms that contribute to an immigrant's inability to assimilate unimpeded and be integrated into American culture (Welch 2003), further fostering an environment of distrust among Americans toward foreigners.

The PATRIOT Act and its subsequent laws aptly demonstrate generalized formal social control but also include a variety of concessions, specifically targeted at immigrants. Although not an overt criminalization, several PATRIOT Act regulations encourage group identity rather than individual conduct for suspicion (Cole 2003). In effect, the protections against terrorism punish immigrants for what they might be suspected of doing rather than for what they have actually done (Welch 2003). The result is an increased and misplaced distrust of immigrants among U.S. citizens, instinctively rendering them suspects of criminal behavior and naturally suspicious by their very nature.

THE "PROBLEM" OF IMMIGRATION

Observing the effects the "war on terror" has had on immigration through the moral panic conception "emphasizes the fact that reactions to unconventional behavior do not arise solely as a consequence of a rational and realistic assessment of the concrete damage that the behavior in question is likely to inflict on the society" (Goode and Ben-Yehuda 1994: 29-30). This study is not about terrorism but rather the after effects and social consequences terrorism has had on immigration since September 11th. With a contentious more recent history of anti-immigration sentiment (Bischoff 2002: 16-18; Hayes 2001: 9-26), formal social controls implemented due to the "war on terror" and prescribed by the PATRIOT Act legislation may be fueling widespread groups of Americans to engage in moral panics against aliens, immigrants, and the foreign-born population.

While the PATRIOT Act's regulations are aimed at controlling immigrants and foreign visitors, recent poll data have indicated that there is a, "significant level of anxiety among Americans that the act and the broader war on terrorism contained potential threats to [their] civil rights and liberties" (Kettl 2004: 104). It is this sentiment that further increases the "effect of unambiguous, collective self-identities" (Doty 2003: 18); further demarcating immigrants and non-citizens from the rest of society.

Although there have been other suggestions that moral panics against immigrants occurred due to the implementation of the late 1990s legislation, there may be a recurring panic against immigration, launched since 9/11 and the inception of the PATRIOT Act. Welch (2002) recognized that moral panics against immigrants began in the early 1990s, led to the harsh 1996 legislation regarding immigration, and then subsided in 1999 (p. 28). It is evident that ideal conditions manifested in the early 1990 as all the moral panic components were in place, including:

> First, the so-called problem of immigration was created according to a collective definition along with several claims-making activities that warned about the putative threat from immigrants. Second, demands, particularly in the form of proposed legislation, were put forth to remedy the problem of immigration. Third, public opinion supported by the perception that immigration was a social problem requiring revised laws and additional measure of social control. Fourth, the media offered heightened attention to those developments, thus amplifying moral panic over immigrants, contributing to its consensus, disproportionality, and volatility. (Welch 2002: 37)

Likewise, the September 11th attacks on the U.S. may have produced similar conditions, perhaps fueling another moral panic against immigrants and foreign-born residents that began with the inception of the PATRIOT Act and continues to this day.

As significant components of moral panics, there is an important relationship between government and media influence, social perception, and collective action, (Hier 2002a: 313) which may be evident in U.S. society since on September 11th, 2001. Using the moral panic model, the trend of general suspicion and criminalization of the foreign-born population in post-September 11th U.S. society are illuminated. Each indicator of the model's indicators can be expounded on and investigated through post-9/11 public opinion polls, federal immigration statistics, and document analyses from several popular printed media, to determine any indication of a shift from social control to moral panics in U.S. society's "war on terror" environment.

CHAPTER 3

Setting the Stage: Ideal Conditions for Panic

Although illegal immigration continues to be a challenging social issue, legal immigration garners as much attention, if not more attention, in the form of regulatory provisos and formal social controls. With regard to the current social climate, several of the moral panic indicators may be evident as a societal panic against undocumented or illegal immigrants is mounting but at the same time, legal immigration is clustered into the same general category of immigration.

Given the fact that there are currently an estimated 11.5 million illegal immigrants in the country (Batalova and Lee 2012), with 481,948 new arrivals in 2011 (Monger and Yankay 2012), the public's concern over the presence of immigrants in the country and urgency to expel them may be impetuous. With regard to legal immigration, it is anticipated that there has been some change in the overall numbers of new immigrants, particularly from countries suspected of propagating *folk devils*. Essentially, sudden, increased concerns over issues that have long been "problems" in society characterizes the moral panic environment; and may now be the case with immigration, both legal and illegal.

Panics are indicated as "the attention paid to a given condition at one point in time is vastly greater than that paid to it during a previous or later time without any corresponding increase in objective seriousness" (Goode and Ben-Yehuda

1994: 44); in essence, a sudden, spontaneous rise in concern that is not spurred by any parallel or society changing event(s) that are taking place. With the constant looming enactment of federal legislation targeting illegal immigration, national protest, rallies, and other public gatherings have become commonplace throughout society although, it is anticipated that the number of both legal and illegal aliens entering the country each year has not changed suddenly or drastically. By the same token, there have not been any recent "events" that should vastly raise the attention given to legal immigrants, in terms of security breaches, terrorist attacks, or additional legislation intended to reduce immigration levels.

With regard to social control, the PATRIOT Act effectively manages the number of immigrants entering into the country by increasing the minimum requirements for workers and lengthening the visa processing time. In addition to the extra security measures implemented for foreign visitors and immigrants, a more comprehensive administrative process was added for work and student visas. Increasing the number of 'filters' applications must go through, the PATRIOT Act may have effectively delayed the number of visas issued, thus hindering the ability of foreigners to legally become part of U.S. society.

MORAL PANICS

Aiding in the determination of moral panics, the publics' opinion and sentiment toward immigrants during the episode must be measured. Therefore, poll data can be used to gauge changes in the level of support for immigration and the types of immigrants that are "accepted" by the public and also, whether or not immigration has become a greater cause for concern among the general public. In a claims making role, the federal government's reaction during a moral panic can be measured through their formal social control function. In this case, the number of legal permanent resident approvals was analyzed, observing the fluctuations and number of issuances, in addition to the changes in category or type, ultimately revealing the types of immigrants that may be subjected to additional and increased control in the post-9/11 society. These measures in turn answered the questions: Are fewer U.S. immigration approvals granted to foreign applicants since 9/11? Has the number of visas issued in each immigration category changed since 9/11? If so, what changes are evident? Have the number of visas issued to particular regions changed since 9/11? If so, which regions have experienced these changes?

THE SEARCH FOR "FOLK DEVILS" IN CONTEMPORARY SOCIETY

In order to identify a general distrust of foreign-born visitors and immigrants, a further specification of the groups that are denied entry to the U.S. may more precisely indicate an enemy, or "folk devil". Though it is difficult to measure the degree to which foreigners may be considered as such, the various labels placed on foreign visitors and immigrants may shed some light into

Table 3.1. Moral Panic Indicators, Outcomes, and Measures

Indicator	Outcome	Measurement
Concern	Heightened anxiety	• Poll data • Document analysis
Consensus	Widespread agreement	• Poll data • Document analysis
Disproporti-onality	Exaggerated threat claims and public concern	• Poll data • Document analysis • Federal statistics
Hostility	Labeling of a "folk devil"	• Poll data • Document analysis
Volatility	Sudden eruption and lingering social controls	• Federal statistics

their level of acceptance in a given society. With regard to immigration statistics, the number and changes in granting approvals to particular categories and geographic regions can also be considered as a means to determine the changes and/or targeted groups of immigrants subjected to moral panics. Finally, poll data illuminates the general attitude towards immigrants and the extent of hostility, marked by support level, usually inflicted upon *folk devils.* Using the moral panic model, each element of moral panics can be explored using a combination of methods (both quantitative and qualitative) to illuminate trends and outcomes (*See* Table 3.1).

Operational Definitions

Given that the expression of criminality is not necessarily used overtly to describe immigrants, a relationship linking the two terms must logically be pursued. Therefore, criminalization refers to the notion of suspicion of immigrants considered deviant or tending toward criminal behavior. In support of the notion of moral panics for this analysis, document analyses using the LexisNexis database of regional newspaper sources was used to illuminate the types, by region, of implied criminality. The connection between foreign-born/descent and criminality was utilized to illuminate media statements that related the two. The use of the term *foreign-born* indicates that the subject is an immigrant or foreign visitor whereas the term *descent* also suggests foreign lineage or a non-U.S., *outsider* reference. These media analyses are explored both quantitatively and qualitatively. The frequency of reports linking foreign-born/descent as it is related to criminality, in the context of post-9/11 society articles sought evidence of overt support for the notion of criminality directed at immigrants from particular countries or with a particular ethnicity. Therefore, the usage and combination of these terms since September 11th, may suggest to readers that identifiable and explicit countries, ethnicities, and types of immigrants are in fact associated with criminality.

The notion of criminalization is further explored with poll and federal immigration data by comparing pre and post September 11th figures. Relying on the 9/11 terrorist attacks and the subsequent implementation of the PATRIOT Act as the turning point, pre and post-9/11 era observations of shifts in attitudes and opinions towards immigrants and changes in visa granting and immigration document approvals are noted. Although a level of suspicion may not be measured with the proposed document analyses independently, the instruments in concert with federal immigrations statistics and polls reveal the public's declining support for immigration, a federally induced reduction in immigration, and a broadened and increased media campaign targeting foreign-born and people of foreign descent; thus implying criminality and therefore indicating an overall criminalization of immigrants.

DOCUMENT ANALYSIS

For the document analyses, this study utilized material from printed media sources. Using the search engine LexisNexis, the printed media employed are routinely accredited with providing broad coverage of national issues and are categorized as general news and can be qualitatively analyzed. Qualitative analyses of media coverage using two separate time spans indicating pre and post September 11th, 2001 periods was selected for several reasons. First, the year 1996 marks the last year that major changes were made to federal immigration laws therefore the "pre" period began on September 11, 1996. Second, September 10th, 2001 was used as the midpoint of data collection and is the day before the 9/11 terrorist attacks took place, perhaps serving as a catalyst or marking the time that the moral panic or criminalization of immigration in America formally began. Lastly, there have been no major additional terrorist attacks on the United States since September 11th 2001 and no major changes to immigration law with 5 years of the November 2001 implementation of the USA PATRIOT Act therefore; no additional negative attention or objective seriousness over concern for immigration should be been evident. The "post" period thus ended on September 10, 2006 to arrive at an even 10-year period under study.

Using the two 5-year pre and post period increments, the LexisNexis database was searched using keywords 'foreign-born', to indicate an immigrant and/or foreigner, or 'descent', only as an implication of ethnicity but excluding its usage as a proper name or verb in stories referring to drug use, plane crashes, etc., and 'crim!', a wildcard term that includes criminal, crime, criminality, and crimes. Other exclusions included reader's letters, viewpoints, or opinion pieces; film, book, or character reviews; sources that excluded U.S. references; statistical tables; native American or African-American (indicating a non-foreign-born population), and references to other eras such as WWI or WWII. News sources were categorized into four regional sources including Northeast, Southeast, Midwest, and Western, to examine differences in the dispersion of media with references of criminalization toward immigration.

Once all the initial exclusions were made, each article was evaluated as a negative or non-negative reference and whether or not the primary issue of the article was race/ethnicity. The negative/non-negative reference was used as a quantitative measure to determine the number of stories that cast a negative view of immigrants as opposed to a non-negative view, to include a neutral or positive reference.

The determination of whether or not the primary issue of the article was race was used to qualitatively examine the types of articles that were reported. For example, a report of a hate crime against an immigrant would be coded as a non-negative story where the primary issue was race. Conversely, a report of an arrest that indicated a particular descent or a foreign-born suspect or arrestee was coded as a negative reference where the primary issue of the article was not race/ethnicity. Any reference to a particular race/ethnicity or country was also noted for an additional qualitative analysis. In qualitative terms, the statements may indicate a level of crisis by their frequency of use and reporting. Also, quantitatively, the units employed may discern trends in usage over an extended period of time.

POLL DATA

A comparison of poll figures utilized questions that asked participants' opinions about several issues relating to immigration including: perceived appropriate levels of immigration, numbers and types of immigrants allowed into the U.S. by visa category and country, immigration restrictions and laws, and any other questions relating to the number and types of immigrants that are allowed in the country. Polls were also used to gauge the importance of domestic issues that have included terrorism before and after September 11th, 2001.

In order to establish trend data on public opinion regarding immigration in the U.S., secondary research of the regularly conducted Gallup Polls were studied. Poll data collected during a 10-year span (September 1996 to September 2006) was examined to determine changes in opinions over time. The following questions were used to establish trend data: "what do you think is the most important problem facing the country today"; "should immigration be kept at its present level, increased, or decreased"; "do you think immigration has been a good thing or a bad thing for the United States in the past". Overall, these data aided in establishing the general public's level of support for immigration and any trends or changes in support for immigration in the U.S. over a period of time.

FEDERAL IMMIGRATION STATISTICS

Finally, visa approval and immigration categories by region were examined to determine changes in the approval process for the same pre and post-9/11 time period. The particular types of approvals by category were noted to determine possible trends in criminalization. These figures were compared to both poll and document analysis data.

In cases where fewer immigration documents were granted to particular regions, changes in regions and the types of immigrants approved were identified and compared with pre-September 11th statistics. In the moral panic environment, changes in the issuance of immigration documents to immigrants from particular regions might indicate a perceived increase the criminalization or implication of *folk devil* to immigrants from those regions. In short, through the document analysis, examination of poll data, and federal statistics, moral panic conditions against immigrants in post-9/11 U.S. society was revealed.

CHAPTER 4

Media Portrayals and Criminal Associations

In order to appropriately examine the concern, consensus, disproportionality, hostility, and volatility indicators of moral panics, three different sources of information were employed. A document analysis determined if, where, and when moral panics were indicated in the media, specifically noting the dates, regions indicated, tone of reporting (i.e. negative or non-negative), hate crime occurrences, and immigrant groups referred to in reporting. Therefore, the document analysis was utilized to illuminate four of the five moral panic indicators: concern, consensus, disproportionality, and hostility.

The document analysis examined major news sources for trends and changes in media reports of criminal activity as related to "foreign born" or particular ethnic descendants over a 10 year period, 5 years prior to the attack on September 11th, 2001 and 5 years after the event. Sources from four major U.S. geographical regions were selected to give a comprehensive depiction of changes in reporting by the media throughout the country and also within the individual regions. The assumption was that changes in the number and type of reports would reveal the moral panic indicators of concern, consensus, disproportionality, and hostility, through the frequency and changes in reporting. It was anticipated that this type of document analysis, focusing on several major regional news sources would offer both qualitative and quantitative conclusions.

DATA COLLECTION

The data were drawn from articles published over a 10-year span, using the LexisNexis newspaper database. A guided news search under the general news category "U.S. News" was conducted using four regional news sources, including Midwest Regional Sources, Northeast Regional Sources, Southeast Regional Sources, and Western Regional Sources. There were three search terms used to gather relevant articles: "foreign born", "descent", and "crim!".

The general "foreign born" term was used to capture the comparative changes, pre and post-9/11, in the usage of the term as it related to criminality, elucidating the concern, consensus, and disproportionality indicators. The term "descent" was also used as an alternative to "foreign born" (i.e. the LexisNexis search conducted was "foreign born *or* descent") to determine if particular ethnicities had been singled out or more frequently mentioned as related to criminality, which is indicative of the hostility indicator and further signifies moral panics through the labeling of a specific *folk devil*. The last search term was "crim!" which was used as a wildcard to include articles referring to crime(s), criminal(s), criminality, and discrimination. Finally, the time span searched was narrowed to September 11, 1996 to September 10, 2001, as the pre-9/11 era, and September 11, 2001 to September 10, 2006 to delineate the post-9/11 period of study.

Given that the units of analysis were the articles themselves, rather than just the discrete search terms, each article was evaluated and then categorized individually. Using the selected search terms, several articles were excluded from the data set. Table 4.1 succinctly explains the reasons for the exclusion of articles from the initial search. All relevant articles were within the context of the United States or contained a reference to the U.S. as opposed to being based entirely on events occurring outside of the country or not involving U.S. citizens. Also, by design, all relevant articles included "crim!" and at least one of the other search terms with a direct connection between or relating the terms in the period of study, thus eliminating references to other eras, such as the crimes against people of Japanese descent during WWII internment or, as was the case in several articles, referring to a local ceremony commemorating Armenian genocide that occurred early in the last century.

Table 4.1. Excluded Articles and Reasons for Exclusion

Reason for Exclusion	Explanation
Era	Referring to an event that took place in another era (i.e. WWII)
Verb/Name	The term "descent" used as a verb (i.e. steep descent or descent into bankruptcy) or as a surname
Letters	Remarks are not media commentary but a reader's personal opinion
Review	Film, movie, book, character, TV, or art reviews
Context	Search terms are not related to each other or are referring to another section of the same article (i.e. metaphorical or terms used in separate articles)
Native U.S.	Subjects were not born in a foreign country or are not immigrants (i.e. Native and African Americans)
No U.S. Reference	Events occurred entirely outside of the U.S. or refer to a news report about occurrences outside the U.S. with no U.S. reference or reference to a U.S. citizen
No CRIM! Reference	The search identified other terms with "crim" (i.e. crimson or crimp)

As this study's logical pursuit was of the connection between the immigrant population and references to criminality, all metaphorical references to "crim!" were also excluded from the data set. The most frequent metaphorical reference included the reference to a professional title of foreign born individuals as, for example, a criminal defense attorney. Alternatively, some articles referred to a particular city or state as having a rising foreign born population and a general increase in crime rate, and were excluded if the increase in crime was not directly attributed to the referenced immigrant or foreign born population.

In addition, references to Native Americans or African Americans were excluded as these populations are considered native born or a segment of the domestic population as opposed to being foreign born or belonging to immigrant groups. Articles that included reviews of films, books, characters, television programs, or art shows were excluded, as were letters or opinion pieces from readers, since the focus of this study is the examination of media remarks rather than personal commentary or individual perspectives on the issue of immigration. Finally, articles that used "descent" as a verb, such as "descent into oblivion" or if the term was used as a proper name, as in the surname Descent, the articles were also excluded.

Table 4.2 illustrates the total number of articles that resulted from the initial search and the number of relevant articles that were ultimately examined for the study. Using the resulting data set of relevant articles, each article was then further evaluated into three categories. The first category considered was the overall tone of the article and deemed negative or non-negative. If categorized as negative, the article associated the immigrant or group with criminal activity (i.e. committed a crime, arrested for a crime, or suspected in a crime) or had a criminal implication (i.e. referred to foreign born suspects, criminals, prisoners, or illegal aliens and populations).

Alternately, articles that were categorized as non-negative were positive or neutral stories or news reports (i.e. delays in the naturalization process for foreign born people are "due to criminal background checks" or foreign descendants are "attracted to areas with low crime rates") or did not implicate or suggest that the immigrant or referenced group was directly participating in criminal activity (i.e. victim(s) being or fear of being a victim of crime, discrimination, or hate crime or the article discussed some of the general or indirect problems often associated with immigration).

Table 4.2. The Search of Regional News Sources

Articles	Northeast N (%)	Southeast N (%)	Western N (%)	Midwest N (%)	Totals N (%)
Total Pre-9/11	181(100)	151(100)	137(100)	81(100)	550(100)
Relevant	76(42.0)	61(40.4)	64(46.7)	21(25.9)	222(40.4)
Excluded	105(58.0)	90(59.6)	73(53.3)	60(74.1)	328(59.6)
Total Post-9/11	322(100)	264(100)	409(100)	135(100)	1130(100)
Relevant	230(71.4)	167(63.3)	271(66.3)	84(62.2)	752(66.5)
Excluded	92 (28.6)	97 (36.7)	138(33.7)	51(37.7)	378(33.5)
Total Combined Relevant Articles	306(31.4)	228(23.4)	335(34.4)	105(10.8)	974(100)

GENERAL PRE/POST-9/11 REPORTING DIFFERENCES

When compared to the pre-9/11 group there was a vast increase in relevant articles and at the same time, a small increase in excluded articles in the post-9/11 group (See Table 4.2). The dramatic upsurge of 238.7% relevant articles indicates an increased focus of articles relating the criminality terms to the foreign born population after 9/11. With this increase, the disproportionality element of moral panics was evident in reporting as the increase suggests a sudden and probable exaggeration in reporting due to a perceived increase in the criminality of immigrants that was not perceptible prior to 9/11 reporting. It was therefore evident that in the reporting period under study, as Welch (2002) asserted, the potential harm was unduly outweighed by the supposed danger, leading to "disseminating distorted messages to influence public and political opinion" (p. 24), and thus augmenting and fueling the panic, in this case, against immigration.

Further, with the substantial increase in the overall number of relevant post-9/11 articles, the number of excluded articles increased from 328 the pre-9/11 group to just 378 in the post-9/11 group, a difference of just 15.2% or 50 articles. The slight increase in excluded articles also suggests that an overall rise in the publication of articles disproportionately associating immigrants with criminality was in fact evident in the post-9/11 period; further revealing the disproportionality indicator and also revealing the concern indicator. Hence, both results are an indication of the increased threat from the criminal population of immigrants, suggesting a higher potential for criminality among immigrant groups. This result is a classic condition of moral panics where the media has effectively amplified the rising criminality of immigrants, signifying an exaggerated public threat which in turn warrants increased public concern and a subsequent moral panic.

A third indicator that was elucidated by the increase in relevant reporting was consensus which was noted by the regional reporting differences in all 4 distinct geographical categories. The importance of regional differences aids in confirming the consensus indicator by measuring and comparing the pre and pot 9/11 reporting differences that existed across the country. An outcome of vast increases in relevant reporting by region therefore further indicated that the whole country was in fact affected; thus confirming the widespread panicked characteristic of consensus that is requisite in a moral panic environment.

Regional Differences

Regionally, the combined Western and Northwest region reporting accounted for more than 65% of all the relevant articles (See Table 4.2) throughout the period of study while the Southeast region claimed almost 25% of the articles. The Midwest region had the fewest number of articles in both pre and post-9/11 periods, accounting for just over 10% of all the relevant articles. It was evident from the sheer number of relevant articles that the moral panic indicators of concern and consensus, characterized by heightened anxiety and widespread agreement, were evident due to the considerable regionally comparative increases in reporting of immigrants as associated with criminality in the post-9/11 period. These results also suggest that there was a common increase in published articles that made the same connection, indicating an exaggerated threat and increase in public concern over immigrants through the association with criminality. Especially in the Northeast and Western regions, the increase in these types of publications was a strong indication of disproportionality.

Table 4.3. Changes in Articles by Regional Distribution

Total	Northeast	Southeast	Western	Midwest
Pre-9/11	76	61	64	21
Post-9/11	230	167	271	84
Difference in # of articles	+154	+106	+207	+63
% Change	+202.6%	+173.8%	+323.4%	+300.0%

Although the Northeast and Western regions had the largest number of relevant articles in the combined pre and post-9/11 periods, the Western region had the highest comparative increase in articles over the period, followed by the Midwest region, both increasing 300.0% or more (See Table 4.3). It was therefore in these two regions that moral panics were most evident in the printed media for the period of study. However, given the considerable increase in the percentage of articles published in all four regions, the increased media attention given to articles that associated crime with the immigrant population suggested that the concern indicator also remained palpable throughout the country.

Although the consensus element does not require universal agreement to qualify as a moral panic, it must at least be perceived to be a real problem that holds widespread credence, which is alleged to be threatening to society, and thus necessitates some resolution (Cohen 1972; Welch 2002). In addition to the overall number of relevant and excluded articles, significant increases in articles relating criminal activities to the immigrant population were found in all 4 regions (See Table 4.3). This increase therefore indicated the clear presence of consensus, concern, and reinforced the aforementioned disproportionality indicator in all areas, throughout the country. Beginning with the concern indicator, the following two chapters will present samples of individual pre and post-9/11 articles found in the document analysis, providing practical examples of how four of the five moral panic indicators were in fact manifested in the post-9/11 printed media.

CHAPTER 5

Increasing Anxiety

Under routine societal conditions, the general public's opinion on immigration is perceived as a social dilemma that necessitates formal, federal political attention and does not typically garner daily attention or even interest in the media. However, in post-9/11 society, the issue of immigration had moved subtly but unquestionably into the realm of moral panic concern once there was a clear implication by the media of particular groups of foreign folk devils; especially noted by the "panicky reactions or wild fluctuations of concern" (Critcher 2003: 23) that were abruptly evident. The concern indicator was therefore the first inkling of moral panic conditions as the media across the country began to aid in perpetuating a moral panic against immigrants to an exceedingly concerned post-9/11 public.

Within the observed regional news sources, a comparison between pre and post-9/11 media indicated a change in reporting with vast increases in criminal associations between suspects that were foreign-born or of foreign descent. When compared to pre-9/11 levels, it was therefore evident that post-9/11 reporting had experienced substantial increases in references to immigrants associated with criminality. Not only did the media increase the number of negative references to criminality among immigrants or foreign-born residents in reporting, but post-9/11 reporting began to indicate particular groups as targets of concern.

TYPES OF PRE-9/11 REFERENCES

Although there were foreign-born or ethnic references in the pre-9/11 era, the majority were in fact descriptions of suspects for the expressed purpose of identification, to clarify citizenship, or to establish immigration status in pending criminal cases or situations described in the individual articles. In some cases, pre-9/11 articles included reports where immigration, race, and/or ethnicity was the main issue in the article and was mentioned in the title. References were therefore included for legitimate reasons that were for this study, considered as necessary and relevant uses of the reference; often aiding in the clarification of details or descriptions of suspects reported in the article. Segments from the sample articles that typify the use of the foreign-born or descent references in the pre-9/11 articles could therefore be categorized into five common types of references utilized in the articles.

Assisting in Identification

In the pre-9/11 era, most of the articles that included foreign-born or descent references were considered necessary as they added relevant details to the article in substantive ways. The added information in these types of articles therefore could potentially aid the reader in clarifying the identification of the suspect referenced. The following article is representative of how the inclusion of the foreign descent reference enhanced in the identification of the suspects:

> After a three-week lull, investigators believe a band of "traveling criminals" has returned to the area with a vengeance after a rash of brazen housebreaks were reported in Greater Boston this week. Preying primarily on homeowners who leave their dwellings unlocked while they are working outside, the thieves, believed to be of Eastern European descent, are suspected in more than 50 housebreaks this summer. (Tom Farmer, "Police

Warn of Roving Band of Home Burglars", *Boston
Herald*, August 22, 2001, 24)

The reference to European descent thus aided in the description
of the itinerant suspects, given that they had not yet been clearly
identified. By adding the reference, the media could have helped
the public increase their awareness of potential Eastern European
suspects and therefore compelled readers to be more vigilant and
perhaps more attentive with local groups speaking an Eastern
European language, or living in particular neighborhoods where
the referenced ethnic group might reside or be encountered.
With the additional information, the public's vigilance was
increased and could therefore have potentially aided in
identifying the suspects and even helped authorities narrow
down the suspect pool.

Unequal Treatment

Another common reference found in pre-9/11 articles included
"foreign-born" to imply the potential for unequal treatment of
suspects or at trial due to the suspects' foreign extraction:

> The terrorism trial that opened yesterday in Federal
> District Court in Manhattan presents an extraordinary
> challenge to the impartial administration of justice in the
> United States. The four defendants are accused of
> participating in a homicidal conspiracy of terror against
> the United States during much of the last decade,
> including the 1998 bombing of American embassies in
> Kenya and Tanzania. Because the attacks were so
> repugnant, and the defendants are foreign-born, the
> prosecutors and the court bear a special obligation to
> insure that the case is handled fairly and in full
> compliance with the rights that must be accorded to
> every defendant in a criminal case. ("The Embassy
> Bombings Trial", *New York Times*, February 6, 2001,
> Section A; Column 1, 18)

The reference was therefore not indicating that criminality was due to the suspects' foreign status. Instead, it suggested that it could be assumed that given the crime was committed against the United States, the foreign status of the suspects might result in unfair treatment in a United States court and therefore might have some effect on the outcome of the criminal trial.

Hearing Summaries and Case Details

Several articles presented cases where deportation hearings were scheduled for immigrants that had already been convicted of crimes and were simply presenting the case details, for example:

> The Supreme Court marched ahead Wednesday on a course giving state governments more rights, ruling that state workers cannot use an important federal disability-rights law to win money damages for on-the-job discrimination. The court also heard the cases of two foreign-born men convicted of crimes in the United States and set for deportation by the Immigration and Naturalization Service. The two --- from Cambodia and Lithuania --- are being detained by the INS because their home countries will not take them back, and the INS still considers them a threat, even though they have completed their sentences. The court will decide whether such open-ended detention is permissible. ("Court curbs lawsuit options of disabled state employees", *The Atlanta Journal and Constitution*, February 22, 2001, 14A)

Similarly, in cases involving an INS investigation, the reference was likely added to clarify and explain the agency's involvement in the case, for example:

> Two foreign nationals and one resident alien, all suspected in a multi-state check counterfeiting scam, are being held on bonds of $5 million each. Mamoona

Kalsoom, 29, Sherali Ismail Shaikh, 32 and Roseline Gomes, 28, all of Indian descent, are in the Madison County Detention Center in Canton. Checks, currency and bank transaction receipts totaling almost $100,000 have been recovered in the case. More seizures and arrests are expected, Madison Police Lt. Eric C. Palmer said. The three were arrested Friday after Kalsoom allegedly attempted to use a counterfeit check to withdraw funds from a Trustmark Bank branch in Madison. The three are accused of randomly opening a checking or savings account with a cash deposit and later withdrawing money on a bogus check, Palmer said. The Immigration and Naturalization Service and the U.S. Secret Service are assisting in the investigation. INS special agent Richard Bruehl said his agency helped determine the suspects' identity and nationality. He said Kalsoom and Shaikh are in the country on tourist visas. Gomes is a resident alien, or "green card holder," he noted. She gave police a New York address. If convicted, the three could be sentenced to maximum of 15 years each in prison. ("Three Suspected in Multi-State Check Scam Jailed in Madison County", *Associated Press State & Local Wire*, October 17, 2000, State and Regional Section)

Established Foreign Roots

Another type of reference included in the pre-9/11 era was the reported foreign-born status of a criminal suspect used to directly link the suspect to another country or clarify direct ties to their foreign roots. An example of linking foreign roots to a suspect is as follows:

Millionaire investor and fugitive James Vincent Sullivan, sought around the globe in the contract killing of his socialite wife Lita at her Buckhead townhouse in 1987, has obtained an Irish passport, the FBI confirmed.

Authorities have evidence that the Boston native of Irish
descent may have fled at some point to his ancestral
homeland. ("Fugitive wanted in 1987 slaying of
Buckhead wife may have fled to Ireland", *The Atlanta
Journal and Constitution*, January 24, 2001, 3B)

In the above article, the reference to the descent of the suspect
was pertinent given that the suspect was of Irish descent and had
actually obtained a passport, which would have enabled the
suspect to easily flee the United States; linking the acquisition of
the passport to the likelihood of fleeing the country. In this case,
the reference was thus relevant as it suggested that, due entirely
to his lineage; the suspect would have been able to seek refuge
from murder charges in the United States in his Irish ancestral
homeland.

Hate Crimes

Another frequent and relevant example of the pre-9/11
criminal/immigrant link was in the case of hate crimes where the
article was not indicting that an immigrant was suspected in
criminal activity but rather was listed as the victim in the report.
For example:

A white supremacist convicted of attacking a man of
Cuban descent and his son outside a rock concert two
years ago was sentenced to five years in prison. Jules
Fettu, once the Florida leader of the white supremacist
World Church of the Creator, showed no emotion as he
was sentenced Friday for beating and stomping William
Salas, 43, and his son Jesiah, 19. The pair had rejected
the group's fliers after a Megadeth rock concert at the
Sunrise Musical Theatre in August 1997, when the
attack took place. Fettu, 26, though charged with
aggravated battery/hate crime, punishable by up to 30
years in prison, was convicted a lesser charge,
battery/hate crime, punishable by up to five years in

prison and up to a $ 5,000 fine. Before his sentencing, the jury watched a tape of a Geraldo Rivera program, which showed Fettu speaking passionately about the World Church's philosophy of white superiority. The World Church advocates the deportation of Jews, blacks and other minorities. Three other former group members were sentenced earlier this year for their roles in the crime. ("White Supremacist Sentenced to 5 Years", *St. Petersburg Times*, November 21, 1999, 4B)

It may also be noted that in pre-9/11 articles, immigrant groups reported to be victims of hate crimes represented a variety of geographic regions including the most frequent references to Asian and Indian descents but also mentioned were crimes against victims of Hispanic, African, Middle Eastern, Russian, Caribbean, Filipino and even Arab and Jewish descent.

Overall, in pre-9/11 sample articles the media added relevant foreign-born or descent references that did in fact enhance the article and aid in describing related or pertinent details of suspects or cases involved. As a result, there were very few unambiguous implications of criminality attributed to immigrants or those who were foreign-born. Instead, the references used the foreign-born or descent designation to aid in clarifying the immigration status or identification of the criminal suspects or their status, who did happen to be immigrants.

EXAGGERATED POST-9/11 REFERENCES

When compared to pre-9/11 articles, rather than using the immigrant group or descent references for identification or clarification, in the post-9/11 era there was often a more exaggerated implication of guilt or criminality, that was much more distinctly and directly attributed to the suspect's immigration/citizenship, lineage, or place of birth. In fact, in many articles the complete removal of the reference would not change the article in any substantive or descriptive manner. Therefore, in many of the post-9/11 cases, the references were completely immaterial to the article and in fact, often appeared to be extraneous.

Extraneous Information

An example of where there was not any particular link to the suspect's indicated ethnicity in the article was:

> A task force is looking for a man wanted in the June 17, 2001, fatal shooting of one man and the wounding of another outside a bar on East 116th Street in Cleveland. Calvin Morrison, 31, who is of Jamaican descent, has been charged with aggravated murder and felonious assault. He is being sought for shooting Rayan Wilthire, 26, of Cleveland, in the chest and abdomen, police said. A second man, Everet McKnight, 50, of Cleveland, was shot in the left foot. Wilthire and Morrison had been arguing in the Blue Mountain Inn on East 116th Street. They were asked to leave, and the argument continued in a nearby alley as a crowd gathered. Morrison pulled a gun and began firing into the crowd, police said. He ran away after the shooting. Morrison is 5 feet 6 and weighs 185 pounds. He has black hair and brown eyes. He has friends in Jamaican communities throughout the United States and Canada, authorities said. ("Suspect Sought in Killing at Bar", *The Plain Dealer*, August 26, 2002, B2)

In the article, the added "Jamaican descent" reference did not, in any manner further, clarify the identification of the already acknowledged suspect. Although the suspect's descent was given, it did not seem to add to the article in any substantive way as was observed in pre-9/11 articles. If the victim's ethnicity was also indicated, there may have been some suggestion or practical connection between the Jamaican born suspect and a victim of the same descent. Otherwise, the inclusion of the suspect's ethnicity does not have any obvious relevance to the article and would not change the article if completely removed.

Even at the end of the article, superfluous information about the suspect's friends in several immigrant communities throughout the country and even in a foreign country was included although again, it does not aid in further explaining or narrowing down the suspect's whereabouts or provide any reason for the additional information. Perhaps in mentioning foreign friends and relatives there was an implication of a flight risk but without any further connections or clear explanation of where the suspect was thought to have gone or why the ethnicity of the suspect was an important detail, the reference is ostensibly irrelevant.

Irrelevant Origin

Another example of adding superfluous information was from the following story involving a rowdy sports fan:

> Russian Mikhail Youzhny's big fourth-round upset of No. 2 seed Rafael Nadal yesterday resulted in the arrest of a 22-year-old Russian reveler swept up by the moment. Moments after Youzhny's victory, Alex Azrilevich, 22, ran onto the court while Nadal was giving his post-match interview and started celebrating. The Holland, PA., resident of Russian descent was arrested by Queens police and charged with "interference of a professional sports event and criminal trespassing," according to Queens police. There were no injuries. (Marc Berman, "Youzhny Fan Arrested", *New York Post*, September 7, 2006, 78)

The article above relayed the arrest of a fan at a sporting event, where again; the ethnic origin of the arrestee was completely irrelevant to the story and did not enhance the story in any way. Although the player and fan did share a Russian heritage, excluding the reference from the article would not substantively change the story and with its addition, the therefore reference did not further explain the reason for the overzealous actions and seemed misplaced given the fact that extreme behavior is common at sporting events and is indicative of a sports fanatic's conduct.

Unclear Attachment

Another common reporting tactic used the reference "U.S. citizen" but also included their specific ancestral descent. However, adding the suspect's descent did not further explain the connection to the suspect's lineage or make any further clarification as to their country of origin. For example:

> A New Hampshire man wanted in the strangulation deaths of two elderly brothers has decided against returning to the Granite State voluntarily. Uno Kim of Bedford, 43, a U.S. citizen of Korean descent, was arrested last week as he waited in line at John F. Kennedy airport to board a flight to Seoul, South Korea, officials said. Kim is charged with two counts of second-degree murder and one count of robbery in the deaths of Gary Joseph, 78, and Theodore Joseph, 76. The brothers, who lived together in Manchester, were found dead at home Feb. 27. The funeral was held Monday. Kim, who has been jailed in New York, appeared in Queens County Criminal Court yesterday. He is due back there on March 31, unless he changes his mind before then and decides he wants to return to New Hampshire. "He's kind of overwhelmed," said his lawyer, Matthew Jeon. "He does not want to be pressed into doing something, to make a quick decision." Jeon said he believes Kim has been able to speak with his family. ("Man Charged in Deaths of Brothers to Stay in N.Y.", *The Union Leader*, March 6, 2003, A1)

Again, the article included the suspect's descent although the suspect was a U.S. citizen and may not have any direct ties to Korea. In this case, the reference was, seemingly irrelevant and if completely removed from the article, would not have substantively changed the article in any manner. If comparing this reference to the pre-9/11 article that referred to the Irish suspect, the foreign-born status was included because of the passport that was obtained, indicating the potential intent of the suspect to escape to his homeland. The major difference in the post-9/11 article with the Korean reference was that the suspect was in fact a citizen and no mention of the sudden acquisition of a Korean passport or any other tangible tie to Korea was indicated.

General Links to Immigrant Criminality

In the post-9/11 era, the trend toward reporting the status of immigrants of foreign–born suspects that were involved in criminal activity was not as perceptible in the pre-9/11 era. Given the law enforcement focus on immigration and terrorism in the post-9/11 era, it was not surprising that increased reporting on sweeps involving federal immigration agents "rounding up" foreign suspects became frequent in reporting. However, the reports expounding on all the details of the arrests were, in some articles, imprecise numbers of violations and arrestees. This type of reporting leads the reader to guess and potentially exaggerate their assumptions, when actual numbers might be much smaller. The generic reporting of numbers may therefore have resulted in an exaggeration of concern of criminal immigrants among the public. An example of this type of reporting is a follows:

> Federal immigration authorities have rounded up 69 foreign-born cab drivers and private security guards in San Diego in what they said was an effort to ensure the security of this weekend's Super Bowl, officials said today. The three-month sweep apparently did not net any known terrorists, but did find 34 foreigners with prior criminal convictions and dozens of others with visa violations, Immigration and Naturalization Service

officials said. Criminal charges are pending against six people and others face immediate deportation, officials said. The roundup came as the immigration service conducted a nationwide registration program requiring tens of thousands of temporary residents from mostly Muslim countries to appear at I.N.S. offices to be interviewed, fingerprinted and photographed. Hundreds of them have been detained for visa violations and scores will be deported. That program touched off an outcry from Arab-American groups, civil libertarians and immigrants' rights groups. Adele Fasano, the immigration service's San Diego district director, said that the three-month Super Bowl investigation had identified more than 100 people with criminal backgrounds or visa violations at the targeted firms. She said 41 remained at large. She said that the program had made the Super Bowl more secure. "I would say that public safety has been enhanced as a result of our extensive screening of individuals who are non-U.S. citizens and are working in activities related to the Super Bowl, and had access to sensitive areas," Fasano said. ("Cab Drivers and Guards Detained in a Three-Month Immigration Sweep", *The New York Times*, January 25, 2003, 4)

Another general immigrant/criminality link was in articles that effectively lump all immigrants into one criminal category; by equating legal with illegal immigrants and even further combining them into one generic foreign-born category. Although the article does eventually explain that Maryland is one state that does not require proof of legal residency, the reference to "foreign-born" applicants rather than separating the legal and illegal immigrants creates exaggerated concern for immigrants a whole. For example:

A spike in license fraud at Maryland Motor Vehicle Administration branch offices that serve immigrant and illegal alien license applicants has prompted state officials to seek emergency regulations to tighten licensing standards, an agency spokesman said yesterday. MVA spokesman Buel Young said overall license fraud at the agency has increased 253 percent, from 146 cases in 2003 to more than 515 last year. Mr. Young said the increases "are more significant" at the 10 MVA branches that serve foreign-born license applicants, who sometimes try to obtain licenses by presenting fake documents. He did not have specific numbers of cases at those branches, and could not explain what other factors might be at work. License fraud increases are "just one of the things that we track," Mr. Young said. "That was one of the areas where we thought we needed to take a closer look and address the situation to see what could be done to curtail it." The Washington Times reported in May that applications for foreign-born people had doubled in Maryland. Several immigrants pointed to the number of people who apply for licenses in the state when their visas expire or use the addresses of relatives who live in Maryland. License applicants in Maryland must prove age, identity and state residency. Maryland is one of eight states that do not require license applicants to prove they are living in the United States legally. (Keyonna Summers, "Tighter MVA Standards Urged: Driver's License Fraud Soars at Branches that Serve Immigrants", *The Washington Times*, August 30, 2006, B01)

Generally, post-9/11 media reporting more frequently included the immigration status or citizenship of a suspect without any explanation or obvious link as to the relevance of the added reference but certainly with more of an implication of suspicion towards this population when compared to the pre-9/11 reporting. In addition to the foreign-born/criminal link, the media also included many more references to one particular immigrant group in post-9/11 reporting; thus increasing and exaggerating the public's concern.

MANIFESTATION OF THE MIDDLE EASTERN FOLK DEVIL

References to Middle Eastern groups that were virtually non-existent in the pre-9/11 articles became very prevalent in post-9/11, especially in the Western and Northeastern regions (See Figures 5.1 and 5.2). Also noted in post-9/11 reporting were the increases in the number of reports from the Midwest region where pre-9/11 reports peaked at 5 (East) Indian references but nearly tripled that peak level in the Arab or Arabic category and had a seven fold increase in the Middle Eastern category. Although before 9/11 the "Asian descent" group received the second highest number of references, in the post-9/11 period there were far fewer references to "Asian descent" and no references to that category in the Southeast and Midwest regions. Instead, post-9/11 references focused on the more generic and geographically broad groups Middle Eastern, foreign-born/descent, and Arab or Arabic categories.

With regard to particular immigrant groups referenced in relevant articles, it was anticipated that the focus of reporting would be on Middle Eastern descendants where most of the countries of origin are included in the federal government's classification system; thus falling within the African or Asian regions rather than in a unique "Middle Eastern" category. It was also expected that there would be an increase in the number of Middle Eastern countries, the larger geographical area encompassing both North African and Asian countries, specifically referenced in the post-9/11 period.

Figure 5.1: Pre-9/11 Groups by Region

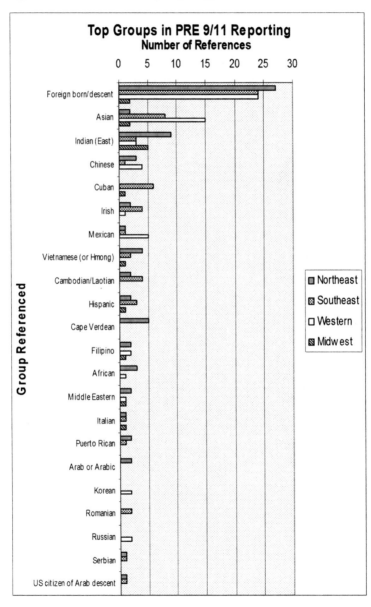

Figure 5.2: Post-9/11 Groups by Region

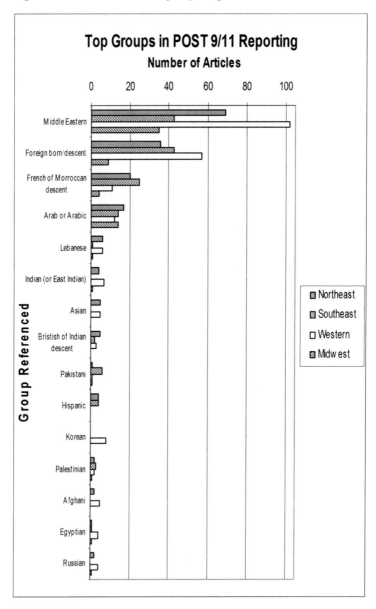

The 9/11 attackers did not ever claim responsibility for the attacks on behalf of any particular country but represented Al-Qaeda conspirators, as part of a terrorist group whose members are traditionally identified as being of Middle Eastern descent. It was therefore expected that an ostensible Middle Eastern "folk devil" would materialize. Interestingly, in the pre-9/11 era, there were 49 different countries or ethnic, racial, or immigrant groups mentioned in the articles whereas 96 different groups were mentioned in the post-9/11 group, an increase of 47 (95.9%) in groups referenced, virtually doubling the number of immigrant group references. With such an increase in the number of groups referenced, immigrant groups became far less broad and actually expanded to include more specific ethnicities and additional countries in a given geographical region (See Figure 5.3). This phenomenon is typical of the concern indicator where heightened anxiety over specific groups becomes more overt and in essence labels an explicit "folk devil".

By incorporating more or expanding the scope of the post-9/11 references, the "folk devil" groups were also extended geographically thus amplifying a more widespread and exaggerated public concern over distinct regions. Although the variance in the number of immigrant groups referenced was evident, comparative changes to the top groups mentioned in each region and the overall combined totals further illustrates the presence of the concern indicator and several other moral panic indicators. In the pre-9/11 era, the most frequently mentioned group was immigrants given the generic label of "foreign-born/descent". By the post-9/11 period, the most common reference was made to "Middle Eastern descent" and to a variety of ethnicities and countries that are habitually included the Middle Eastern region.

The top 10 groups mentioned in the pre-9/11 period had 21 references to 4 diverse geographic regions, defined by the federal regional groupings, including 2 in Africa (no Middle Eastern references), 9 in Asia (including 2 Middle Eastern references), 5 in Europe and 5 in North America (1 article referring to Middle

Figure 5.3: Top 10 Immigrant Groups Referenced

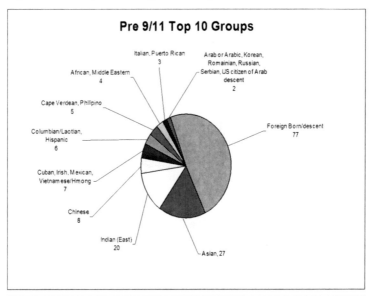

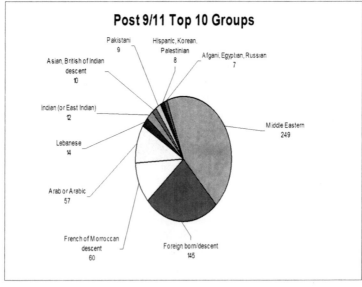

Eastern descent), along with the reference to the more generic "foreign-born/descent" category. The post-9/11 era also referenced the "foreign-born/descent" group and included the same 4 geographic regions but with only 14 regional references. Of the 14 references, 9 were to areas in Asia (including 6 Middle Eastern references), 1 reference to Africa (a Middle Eastern reference), 3 to Europe (but 2 referring to Asian and Middle Eastern descents) and 1 reference to North America.

In essence, the majority of the post-9/11 articles made references that changed the pre-9/11 "Asian region's" dynamic, by expanding the Middle Eastern region, referring to additional countries and ethnicities, and reducing the number of East Asian countries included in the category. In addition, the top few groups referenced, foreign-born or descent, Middle Eastern, and Arab or Arabic categories, were more geographically broadened, effectively expanding the area of possibilities for *folk devils* which now included regions beyond the Middle East and into the more expansive Arab world in addition to the nonspecific but all-encompassing foreign-born group. It is worth noting that in the post-9/11 period of study, all references to (French of) Moroccan descent are attributed to one single individual, Zacarias Moussaoui; the only person indicted and sentenced for conspiracy for his role in the 9/11 attacks (See http://www.usdoj.gov/usao/vae/).

The next chapter will further explore the moral panic indicators of consensus, disproportionality, and hostility found in the document analysis; revealing changes in frequencies of reporting the link between immigrants and criminality, across all geographic boundaries. Also, a continued exploration of the exaggerated threats and claims that have been perpetuated by the post-9/11 media will be pursued.

CHAPTER 6
The Labeling of a Folk Devil

With the concern indicator represented through the media in all regions of the country, moral panic indicators consensus, disproportionality, and hostility were also evident in measurable expressions. Although reporting frequencies had not reached the high levels experienced immediately after the attacks of 9/11, on average, the frequencies have exceeded totals from the post-9/11 period in all regions. These fluctuations have in essence, revealed the presence of the consensus indicator as characterized by widespread agreement in all regions, which was complemented by a display of disproportionality, indicating that the suspect population is both serious and genuine. The height of a panicked environment culminates in the manifestation of hostility or exacting a label on the demonized population. Thus, the collective fear constructs a *folk devil* reviled and endorsed by all three key players in the moral panic environment; the media, government, and public.

REGIONAL FREQUENCIES

The frequency in the number of articles published was higher on average and exhibited more fluctuations in the post-9/11 era in all regional categories (See Figure 6.1), illustrating the consensus, concern, and disproportionality indicators. The Western and Northeastern regions consistently had the highest average number of articles published monthly until 2004, indicating a disproportional number of articles associating immigrants to criminality in these regions and identifying the presence of exaggerated threat claims. In addition, although the Northwestern region had the highest frequency of articles overall, the Western region had the greatest number of fluctuations in published articles through the post-9/11 time frame, with several months having more than 10 articles published each year. Therefore, regionally, the Western media displayed the highest level of anxiety and illustrated the concern indicator.

Figure 6.1: Pre and Post Monthly Frequencies of Articles by Region

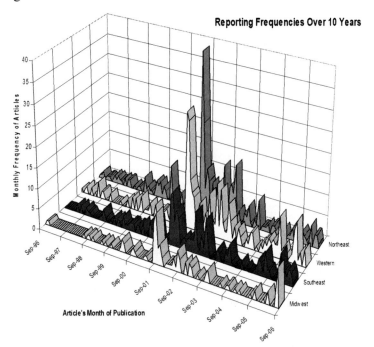

In 2004, the Southeastern and Western regions frequencies began increasing, passing the declining Northeastern frequency in the average number of monthly published articles, until the end of the period of study. Given the increase in all regions in the post-9/11 period, the moral panic indicators of concern and consensus are both indicated and have remained elevated since the 9/11 attacks. Although the volatility indicator was not initially considered as an outcome for the document analysis, the sudden eruption in the frequency of published articles occurring at different times and in different regions throughout the post-9/11 period also typifies a moral panic environment.

TONE AND SUBJECT CHANGES IN REPORTING

Of the relevant articles, each article was first evaluated and categorized as negative or non-negative. In the pre-9/11 time frame, 84 articles were categorized as negative while in the post-9/11 group 389 were categorized as negative, an increase of 305 (363.1%) negative articles. The results for non-negative articles included 93 articles in the pre-9/11 time frame and 279 in the post-9/11 period of study, an increase of 186 (200.0%) non-negative articles. Table 6.1 provides a tabular form of the results of subject and tone reporting.

Table 6.1 Changes in Subject and Tone of Relevant Articles

Categories	Negative	Non-Negative	Immigration IS the primary issue	Immigration is NOT the primary issue	Hate Crimes
Pre-9/11	84	93	147	73	49
Post-9/11	389	279	350	317	188
Difference in # of articles	+305	+186	+203	+244	137
% Change	+363.1	+200.0	+138.1	+334.2	+283.7

The articles in the pre-9/11 were more frequently non-negative and focused on reports where immigration was more often the primary issue in the article, illuminating the concern, consensus, and disproportionality indicators. Also, from the articles under the period of study, it may be noted that reports of hate crimes occurred less frequently in the pre-9/11 era, indicating that there was less widespread anxiety over immigrant groups. In the post-9/11 era, there was a substantial increase in the number of negative articles relating criminality to immigrants, even though the primary issue of the article was not immigration, the articles made reference to an immigrant group even as the reference was not relevant to the article's purpose or meaning. Again, the increase in references to criminality typifies four of the moral panic indicators including: concern, hostility, consensus, and disproportionality.

TIME PERIOD CHANGES

As anticipated, the combined number and frequency of articles (See Figure 6.2) that associated criminality with the foreign born population increased immediately after September 11th, 2001. Articles published over the period of study reached a combined peak in September 2001 with 89. In the post-9/11 era there were few other occasions where sudden increases in the number of published articles rose to 30 or more articles, September 2002, January 2003, and March 2003. By 2006, the end of the period of study, there were 3 months where more than 15 articles were published, 16 in March and April, then reaching as high as 20 in August 2005.

Although there have been no additional major attacks on the U.S. since 9/11 and no new legislation that would affect immigration regulations as significantly as the PATRIOT Act, the impending revisions of immigration laws that will formally address the illegal immigration predicament in the U.S. will certainly have some effect on the types and frequency of articles similar to those under study. As previously mentioned, the negative attention and interest ascribed to illegal immigration is virtually impossible to separate from legal immigration and therefore, legal immigrant groups are often equally affected, negatively or otherwise, by the media spotlight. It was evident that sudden increases in articles that related immigrants to criminality were prevalent during the same time period in all regional sources, which is characteristic of several moral panic indicators.

Figure 6.2: Regionally Combined Number of Articles Published
from September 1996 to September 2006

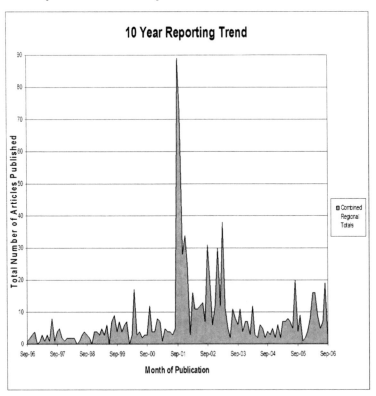

Hate Crime

Another category considered in the document analysis was
whether or not hate crimes were mentioned in the articles. The
articles were categorized as non-negative since hate crimes did
not generally indicate a foreign born person or immigrant as the
perpetrator but rather as a victim of the hate/ethnic/
discriminatory incident. This categorization and subsequent
examination of hate crimes among the relevant articles further
elucidated the moral panic indicators concern, hostility, and

consensus as the panic was directed toward immigrants, indicating them as victims of the panic.

Pre-9/11 articles indicated that hate crime victims were primarily from the Asian region, more specifically, the majority of references were to immigrants of Indian or Asian descent. The number of hate crimes reported in the post-9/11 era increased significantly however the targeted groups were of Asian descent but primarily from Middle Eastern countries with significant numbers mentioning the generic ethnicity of Arab/Arabic descent (See Figure 6.3). Overall, there were 51 references to victimized groups in the pre-9/11 period of study and 234 in the post-9/11 era, indicating a 358.8% increase in the number of hate crimes, clearly an indication of the concern and consensus indicator but also displaying disproportionality in the specific types of groups being victimized. Further, 17 different groups mentioned in the pre-9/11 period and 24 different groups mentioned in the post-9/11 period, there was some increase and also variation in the ethnicities of victimized groups.

One of the new categories that was included in the top groups referenced in the post-9/11 era was "American or U.S. citizens of" varied descents; all of these 11 references included descendants of Asian region countries and ethnicities, and 9 out of the 11 referred to Middle Eastern countries including Iraq, Iran, Lebanon, Palestine, and the more generic Arab or Arabic and Middle Eastern references. In the post-9/11 era the combined top groups mentioned included 24 named groups, again, most of which are considered as part of the Asian region and are often referred to as Middle Eastern groups. All regions had Middle Eastern and Arab or Arabic as the top two groups referenced as victims in post-9/11 articles mentioning hate crimes. Specifically targeting the Middle Eastern groups as the most recurrent victims of hate crime displays the hostility indicator by clearly defining the immigrant group that was most frequently labeled as *folk devils*.

Figure 6.3: Hate Crime Victimization Reported in Pre and Post-9/11 Articles

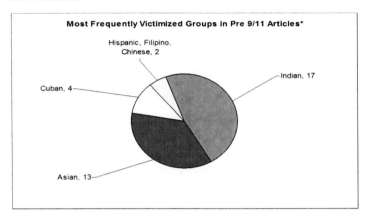

Most Frequently Victimized Groups in Pre 9/11 Articles*

*The remaining groups had 1 reference each: African, Arab, Bangladeshi, foreign born, immigrants, Indo-Caribbean, Japanese, Middle Eastern, Palestinian, Russian, and Syrian. One of the articles mentioned 3 different ethnic groups.

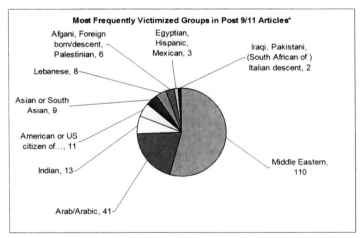

Most Frequently Victimized Groups in Post 9/11 Articles*

*The remaining groups had 1 reference each: Arab of Moroccan descent, French, Iranian, Jordanian, Moroccan, Muslim, Portuguese, Russian, and Syrian.

MEDIA ANALYSIS

In examining the changes to the media portrayal of immigrants, it is evident that an increase in overall reporting of immigrant activities, in association with criminality, and the frequency of criminal activity attributed to immigrants was supported in post-9/11. Therefore, in its claims making role, the media successfully propelled the conception of specifically named immigrant groups as *folk devils* to the forefront of reporting. The post-9/11 era included in this study was therefore fraught with articles and stories that did not shed a positive or "moral" light on immigrants in general. Instead, a subtle connection between criminality and immigrants was created, potentially labeling the immigrant population as legitimate source of fear and even suspicion among citizens.

The Media's Criminal Connections

With the increase in the media reporting of criminality as it related to immigrants in the post-9/11 era, as noted in Figures 6.1 and 6.2, it was evident that the media had indeed played a major role in making and subsequently strengthening the connection between immigrants and criminals. Although the search terms used for this analysis were limited to just a few possibilities, the sheer change in the number of articles linking criminality to the foreign-born populace does indeed indicate that there was some level of general suspicion or mistrust directed toward immigrant groups by segments of the media in all observed regions across the country.

Moreover, the post-9/11 drop in the number of excluded articles was an indication that when reports of immigrants were printed, they were more likely to contain references to criminality in the post-9/11 media and therefore considered relevant to the study. Although there was variation in the actual number of relevant articles in each geographical region, it was apparent that immigration issues as related to criminal activity became more "newsworthy" after the attacks on September 11th;

mimicking the general overall increase in media attention as observed in previous moral panics and thus elevating the panic to the national level. Accordingly, not only was the immigrant population receiving more press in the post-9/11 era under study, but the press they were receiving was more often relating them, in some way, to criminality; effectively labeling them as "enemies" to the public; or in moral panic terms *folk devils*.

The Government's Criminal Connections

Given the new reporting post-9/11 trend among the media and the subsequent reaction from the public, the third ingredient of the moral panic environment was manifested where "the effort to focus central control against the 'enemy' [was] relentlessly pursued by strong proponents of social control" (Altheide 2006: 27); in this case, the federal government in its claims making role through the passage of new federal social control regulations.

Throughout history, several eras have in fact have had "enemies" and the corresponding government, their own blameworthy immigrant populace; from the Japanese Americans in WWII to the red scare and the Russians during the Cold War. Therefore, with the support of the federal government, society continues the task of constructing similar "enemy" claims through media reporting that effectively propagates and amplifies the notion (Altheide 2002) that enemies are first visually identifiable and second, seemingly everywhere. This belief was in fact pursued and sustained by claims makers (i.e. the federal government and the media) and marked by identifiable and specified *folk devils* in the in post-9/11 moral panic environment's reporting.

A Criminal Connection

In the post-9/11 era, criminal connections made in the moral panic environment are fairly arbitrary in the sense that an individual's ethnicity is not always obvious and most people would in fact not necessarily be unable to identify the ethnicity of an individual by sight, without any prior knowledge of that individual. In post-9/11 reporting, the identifiable enemy that was both targeted as a victim and most often mentioned in reporting was "Middle Eastern" which is misnomer. This is due to the fact that the term "Middle Eastern" refers to a region rather than country that includes a widely varied population of cultures and ethnicities that are extremely diverse and vastly different from each other, in physical features, language, dress, and customs. With such varied features among the Middle Eastern population, it is therefore particularly difficult to distinguish and readily demarcate their differences. These vast differences result in an exceptionally general targeted *folk devil* that includes a wide geographic population, affecting many other ethnicities and immigrant groups that are within the general population.

Another one of the top named "enemies" in post-9/11 reporting was also a misnomer, referencing the term Arabic or Arab. Defining the term Arab or Arabic is not exacting and usually requires some reference to a combination of language, culture, and linage. Most often, the term Arab generally refers to a group of people that speak a particular language where visual identity has no direct link to language except the group includes people that are primarily inhabitants of Southwest Asia and North Africa that may share some common physical features. Consequently, an accurate visual identification cannot easily be made of an Arab or Arabic person.

An additional interesting development in the groups named in post-9/11 reporting was the fact that the references became much less diverse, focusing on the Middle Eastern regions and the Arabic speaking segments of Asia and Africa. The groups of enemies therefore became less varied and focused instead on one region in the post-9/11 era when compared to pre-9/11 groups mentioned in reporting, which included groups from all different parts of the world. The general category of "foreign born/descent" remained high in both pre and post-9/11 displaying the continued and general distrust of immigrants, although again, visually, an immigrant is not readily identifiable although many of the reports indicated criminality of an individual that "appeared to be foreign born" or of "foreign descent".

The result of post-9/11 reporting effectively convinced the public to accept the named *folk devils*, which in turn aided in the increase of the government's ability to sustain and successfully impose formal social controls (i.e. PATRIOT Act) that targeted the identified criminal population but also greatly affected the general public. With the government as a strong basis of support, the media in a moral panic environment is free to make clear, criminal connections for the public in its reporting. Thus, the government and media together may augment and strengthen both formal and informal means of social control against the acknowledged and frequently vilified population while simultaneously gaining the support and cooperation of the general public.

The media's ability in a moral panic environment to effectively propel a particular group of people into a demonized category, discordantly targeted by society, is not an unfamiliar trend. In fact, the media must excel in creating a widely accepted "folk devil" and subsequently drive that named group to the forefront of reporting in order to successfully induce a moral panic. Although not referring specifically to a moral panic situation, Kearney (1999) noted the media's exceptional ability wherein:

> The tendency of media hype, so prone to hysteria, is to anathemise anything that is unfamiliar as 'evil'. The 'other' thus becomes the 'alien', the stranger the scapegoat, the dissenter the devil. And it is this proclivity to demonise alterity as a threat to our collective identity which so easily issues in paranoid fantasies about invading enemies. (p. 258)

It was exactly these conditions that existed in the post-9/11 environment; thus allowing the media to begin a campaign to generate a moral panic against clearly defined immigrant groups.

The next chapter will continue to explore the extent of moral panics in U.S. society through an examination of poll data that was collected throughout the period of study. These data will further elucidate several moral panic indicators and demarcate the level of apprehension the public has experienced towards immigration and the related issues of national security and terrorism. Finally, polls gauging public approval of the levels of immigration will be considered as a means to determine the general endorsement and support for immigration.

CHAPTER 7

Heightened Concern and Impetuous Threats

As the second source of information, this investigation relied on an exploration of three public opinion polls that were employed to further examine the reaction of the citizenry towards immigrant groups, before and after September 11th, 2001. Given that polls are based on a sample of the adult population, it was anticipated that exploring several poll issues related to immigration would provide evidence of a broad consensus within the general population. This method therefore directly addresses the concern, hostility, consensus, and disproportionality indicators found in the moral panics conception, throughout the period of study.

Before and after the September 11th terrorist attacks, numerous national polls (i.e. Gallup, Pew, RAND, etc.) were conducted to determine the American public's opinions on a variety of domestic issues. Following the time frame of the document analysis, pre and post-9/11 time periods of study, monthly published polls were evaluated to measure the degree of change in opinions on immigration and related domestic issues that are commonly associated with foreign visitors and immigrants in society. Trends and changes in public opinions were especially noted and compared to illustrate the presence of the same four indicators of moral panics that were examined in the document analysis.

"MOST IMPORTANT PROBLEM" POLL

Using the reference search from in the LexisNexis database, polls and surveys related to "social problems" were identified. The search was narrowed to the poll question "what do you think is the most important problem facing this country today?". The search for relevant poll data was further narrowed to include only Gallup polls that were taken during the 9/11/96 to 09/10/06 period of study. The search yielded 70 polls taken by the Gallup Poll Organization, conducted through regular telephone interviews over a 3 to 4 day period, and soliciting responses from a national adult sample over the 10-year span.

The 70 polls were considered but 4 were excluded because the date range of the poll was out of the period of study, the poll question was worded differently, or the same poll was published more than once. The average number of participants per poll throughout the 10-year span was 1,009 adults per poll. Poll publication dates included in the period of study began on January 13th 1997 and ended on August 15th 2006. Participants were able to give multiple responses to the selected poll question.

Although there were a range of issues offered in response to the poll question, for this examination, 3 issues that are most closely related to concerns routinely associated with immigration were considered: terrorism; national security; and immigration/illegal aliens. A summary of poll responses evoking these 3 issues and given within the period of study are provided in Figure 7.1. Poll responses were recorded as the percentage of respondents reporting a particular issue as the "most important problem facing the country today".

Within the three chosen categories, terrorism was not given as a response until the October 18, 2001 poll. However, there were pre-9/11 variations on the terrorism responses, given on 2 occasions, including terrorism/national security as 1% of the responses in January 1999 and terrorism/TWA plane crash as 6% of the responses in 1996. The "terrorism" response peaked in the October 18th 2001 poll, claiming 46% of the responses and

Figure 7.1: Most Important Problem Poll

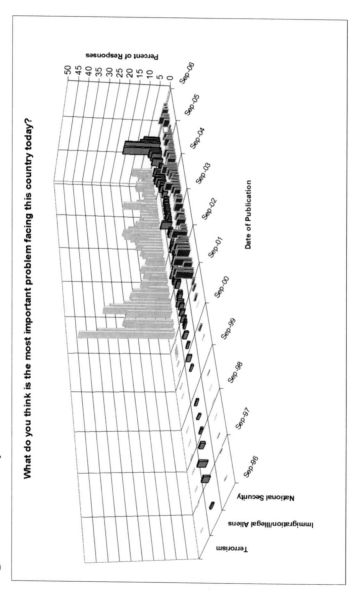

What do you think is the most important problem facing this country today?

continued by maintaining more than 20% of the responses until September 18th 2002. The terrorism response, which had been at the highest level immediately following 9/11, up to 46% in October 2001, dropped, then fluctuated throughout 2002 till 2005 finally declining to as low as 3% of the responses by June 2006.

Participants responding "national security" to the poll question reached a peak of 8% in February 2002 and then fluctuated between 7% and less than 0.5% for the remainder of the post-9/11 time frame. It was anticipated that immediately after 9/11, both terrorism and national security responses would be more frequently selected as the "most important problem" however, immigration did not actually peak until the middle of 2006 with 19% of the responses in April and 18% in June. As the end of the period of study approached, the immigration/illegal aliens' category of responses continued an upward trend, reaching the highest levels of nearly 20% in 2006, while the number of both national security and terrorism responses continued to decrease.

When contrasted with the pre-9/11 responses, the percentage of respondents indicating terrorism as the "most important problem" rose significantly in 2001 immediately after the attacks of 9/11 and on average, both the immigration/illegal aliens and national security responses displayed sustained comparative increases in the post-9/11 period. National security responses were more frequently indicated as the "most important problem" when compared to immigration/illegal alien responses until April of 2006 when the number of respondents selecting immigration/illegal aliens exceeded the preceding highest percentage totals of national security responses by 111.1%. The "immigration/illegal aliens" response also surpassed the terrorism response levels, reaching a high of 19% of respondents in April 2006, a level not reached by the terrorism responses since November 2002.

WHO CARES ABOUT TERRORISM OR NATIONAL SECURITY?

Immediately after 9/11, polls indicated that terrorism was indeed one of the greatest concerns among the American public. However, since 9/11, there was in fact a gradual overall decline in the number of pollsters with regard to their level of concern for terrorism. The exception to the overall decline was the few brief increases which perhaps could be attributed to other acts of terrorism around the world that involved American casualties or Al-Qaida links to 9/11.

Examples of brief increases of responses to "terrorism" included periods in March 2004 after the bombings in Madrid which then began to subside shortly after the car bomb at an Egyptian hotel in October of the same year. A second brief rise in "terrorism" responses was indicated in October 2005, beginning in July after the London bombings and eventually subsiding by October after the bombings in Indonesia occurred. These rises were in essence predictable as previous research on public opinion reveals a pattern of focus shifting from external threats shortly after an initial threat has faded, which is then followed by a shift in attention to more proximate problems of a domestic origin (Holsti 1996). This same pattern was evident as the turn towards the issues surrounding internal legal and illegal immigration by the end of the period of study was indeed receiving greater levels of public concern.

Before 9/11, national security was among the lowest issues that captured the concern of pollsters. As was the case with "terrorism" responses, pollster's concern for national security, although never reaching the same high levels of poll responses given for terrorism, had subsided significantly by the end of the period of study. In fact, national security responses never displayed much variance in amplitude except at the initial period marking the pre and post-9/11 era, followed by minor fluctuations throughout the period of study.

In any country following a terrorist attack, anti-terrorist measures usually embrace a predictable governmental response that includes a hasty set of emergency provisions, designed to enhance security but also used as a means to show that politicians and legislatures are taking some form of practical action in response to both media and public outcries (Thomas 2002). Given the comparative rise in pre and post-9/11 concern for the issues of terrorism and national security, it appears that after a marked rise in concern for these issues, the public's focus shifted to the escalating indigenous problem of immigration; with so called "illegal immigration" gaining the bulk of the government, media, and public's attention.

Perhaps, as Welch (2006) asserted, as is often the case in a moral panic, the fear of terrorism and national security may in fact proliferate so much that it undercuts most of the rational and impartial treatment of immigrants (p. 101). The end result is public hostility that is habitually aimed at particular "other" groups which simply and predictably ends up to be non-citizens and immigrants of all descriptions.

"GOOD THING/BAD THING" POLLS

The second poll results examined were taken from the Gallup poll, asking the question "on the whole (or generally speaking), do you think immigration is a good thing or a bad thing for this country today?" (See Figure 7.2). Although the polls for the period of study were not as frequently conducted, overall trends were examined from the results. Included in these results were 6 polls, with the first poll conducted in June 1997. While the percentage of those polled responding "good" and "bad" was almost even at the beginning of the period of study, the two response trends moved in opposite directions until the second poll was conducted in July 2001. The number of respondents indicating "mixed" and "no opinion" on the poll was negligible therefore; the results of the polls indicate an inverse relationship between the good and bad responses throughout the period of study.

CHANGES IN LEGAL IMMIGRATION LEVELS

The third poll examined during the period of study asked participants, "Should legal immigration into the U.S. be kept at its present level, increased, or decreased?" The average number of participants per poll was 1,568 using a national adult sample. All polls were conducted using the telephone interviews except the poll conducted on October 2nd, 2002, where 400 of the 3,262 adults polled were conducted as face to face interviews. Only one poll, in October 1996 was conducted in the pre-9/11 period of study while 14 polls were conducted in the post-9/11 time frame, with the first poll after the September 11th attacks published on September 15th, 2001 and the last on May 9th, 2006.

Figure 7.2: Good Thing/Bad Thing Poll

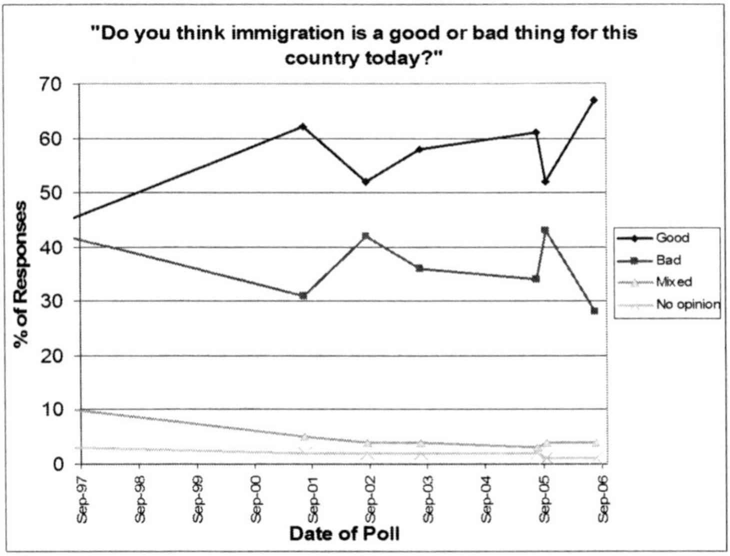

Although only one poll was conducted in the pre-9/11 era, the trend in support for the decrease of immigration levels began at 50% in 1996 and reached a peak of 57% in support of a decrease in immigration levels in September 2001. Overall, the percentage of respondents indicating support for a decrease in immigration levels consistently claimed the largest percentage of respondents, indicated by over 40% of the respondents in 12 out of the 15 polls (See Figure 7.3). The category claiming the second largest levels of support was the "present level" group, claiming more than 30% of participant responses in 11 out of the 15 polls. Both of these trends indicate that the public was not generally inclined to support changes in legal immigration levels and was perhaps more inclined to reduce immigration levels, especially after 9/11. Further, the data indicated three significant and sudden drops in the "decrease" category between 2002 and 2004, in 2005, and in April 2006.

Figure 7.3: Changes in Legal Immigration Levels

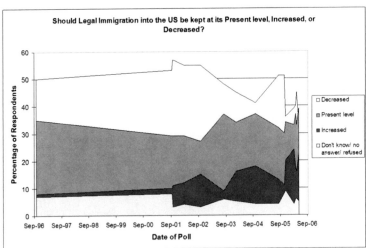

The moral panic indicators of concern, hostility, consensus, and disproportionality as related to immigration/illegal aliens were not exhibited immediately following 9/11, as were the terrorism and national security responses. However, beginning in late 2005, responses in this category began increasing and actually exceeded the terrorism and national security indicators by April 2006. Again, no additional attacks have occurred in the U.S. since 9/11 but in observing comparative changes in the pre/post period of study, concern, consensus, and disproportionality indicators were present beginning with the 2006 polls without any tangible or additional significant changes to U.S. immigration.

Throughout the period of study, respondents supporting a decrease in legal immigration averaged 47%, those in support of maintaining the "present level" of immigration averaged 33%, those supporting an increase averaged only 15%, and those responding "don't know, no answer, or refused to respond" averaged just 5%. Sharp changes in the all the participants' responses occurred between October 2005 and the middle of 2006, especially in the November 2005 poll and again between March and April of 2006. These abrupt changes in responses indicated heightened levels of anxiety and apprehension towards immigration in general, which in a moral panic environment typify both the concern and disproportionality indicators.

As anticipated, the number of participants responding that immigration is a "bad thing" increased immediately after 9/11, indicating that the public generally concurred that immigration was perhaps a rising domestic problem as observed through the decline in levels of public support for immigration. The trend represents some of the changes after 9/11 that are indicative of the moral panic indicators concern, consensus, and disproportionality. After support levels slowly increased until July of 2005, there was another increase in respondents indicating that immigration was a "bad thing" by September 2005. The results illustrate a sudden rise in concern without any rise in "objective seriousness" that is typically observed in the moral panic environment.

Given the fact that the attackers were initially admitted into the country legally and that there have been no major attacks since 9/11, the level of general concern for immigration although initially logical, has over time become unfortunate for the vast number of legal immigrants with honorable intentions.

Therefore, in response to the moral panic environment and rising public concern over immigration there has also been a distinct movement from a variety of citizen and immigration reform groups pleading for national policy changes to the existing, and ostensibly inadequate, U.S. immigration system.

THE ENDURING AND INCREASING CONCERN OVER IMMIGRATION

Initially, apprehension over immigration was not high among pollsters but continued to increase and eventually became one of the pollsters' major issues of concern, rising to over 15% of the respondents in the last few months of the period under study. The indicators of concern, hostility, consensus, and disproportionality with regard to immigration were therefore more evident at the end of the period of study, when compared to the immediate post-9/11 reaction of pollsters.

Since 9/11, legal immigration has received several added security measures that have resulted in a more protracted and complex route for immigrants seeking to obtain legal permanent residency or citizenship, and even to acquire a more temporary status like a student visa (through SEVIS) or short term visitor's visa (from US VISIT). The measures may have indeed contributed to a strengthening of national security; however, they have also greatly contributed to the inadvertent criminalization of legal immigration. With legal immigration since 9/11 under more severe scrutiny, very little has been done to curb the so-called "illegal immigration" problem that presently subsists in the U.S.; thus coalescing and giving undue and excessive negative attention to immigration as a whole. In reality, these two forms of migration are entirely different in purpose, intent, and objective and should therefore never be placed under a single, general immigration category, as is regrettably and typically the case.

Although there is no simple solution to the challenges of creating a non-discriminatory and equitable immigration system, steps should be taken by both the government and the media to publically ensure that the legal immigrants are not routinely lumped together in the same criminal category as illegal migrants. The definition of immigration should, in all cases, imply and signify only the legal methods of granting permanent residency or citizenship. However, in post-9/11 society, the public's sentiment towards immigration remains too broad and attached to the negative connotation of immigration proclaiming that:

> [W]e have new laws, new agencies, and lots of new government spending to fight off foreign invaders. But our immigration policies [continue to] leave the door to our nation open wide to the world's law-breakers and evildoers. (Malkin 2006: 98)

In fundamental terms, as long as the present number of migrant workers illegally entering the United States continues to grow, the perceived "problem" of immigration will persist to remain a significant and ongoing concern in the public's opinion. In addition, with the stricter immigration measures imposed by legislation such as the PATRIOT Act, it is evident that:

> [W]e now find the imposition of more intensive regimes of regulation, inspection, and control and in the process, our civic culture becomes increasingly less tolerant and inclusive, increasingly less capable of trust. (Garland 2001: 194-195)

The next chapter will continue to explore the extent of moral panics in U.S. society through an examination of relevant federal immigration statistics on legal permanent resident (LPR) approvals. These data will examine the disproportionality and volatility indicators as a means to measure the federal response to immigration by comparing changes in LPR issuances over the period of study, by both applicant category and region.

CHAPTER 8

Immigration Anxiety: The Federal Response

With the results from the media analysis as a guide, the last source of information employed in this analysis was federal immigration statistics, used to investigate issuances and approvals of the federal government's Legal Permanent Resident (LPR) in all six regional categories and five major classifications. These analyses were used to determine which regions and categories of immigrants were most affected in the post-9/11 era due to new federal initiatives and legislation, such as the PATRIOT Act and other associated regulations. The exploration focused on the disproportionality and volatility indicators characteristic of a moral panic environment.

In examining federal immigration statistics, fluctuations and trends marked by the number and types of immigration approvals granted after the attacks of September 11th 2001, were explored to determine the degree of disproportionality and existence of volatility indicators generated from the new immigration regulations primarily spawning from the PATRIOT Act. More specifically, an examination of the legal permanent resident (LPR) or "green card" approvals, including observed changes in the number of issuances to the major geographical regions and approval patterns by immigration category, was utilized. This study included all available LPR issuances reported by the U.S. Department of Homeland Security (DHS) from 1996 to 2006, with 2006 figures being released and made available to the public in April 2007.

There are 6 major geographical regions the federal government uses to classify immigrants entering the country: Africa; Asia; Europe; North America (includes the Caribbean and Central America); Oceania (includes Australia); and South America. For immigrants seeking LPR status there are also 5 major classifications that immigrants may petition under: family sponsored preferences; employment based preferences; immediate relatives of U.S. citizens; diversity programs; and refugee and asylee adjustments.

The LPR data were chosen for this study as the initial requirements, application, and approval process provides the most rigorous scrutiny for immigrants when considering the length of time between application and approval, scope and extent of background checks, and variety and volume of requisite documentation. Of all the possible immigration categories and processes, it is therefore the LPR approval process and regulations that have been most affected by the implementation of the PATRIOT Act.

As the granting of LPRs is a continuous process, it was logically assumed that changes due to the implementation of the PATRIOT Act and other new federal regulations would not take full effect immediately following the attacks on September 11th 2001. After major adjustments in the 1996 federal immigration regulations, it took between two and three years for LPR issuing patterns to exhibit changes in approval levels and ultimately reach the lowest issuance levels in all regions. In examining the post-9/11 period under study, 2003 marked the lowest approval level for LPRs granted in all the immigration categories (See Figure 8.1). Therefore, after the implementation of the PATRIOT Act, approval levels exhibited an approximately two year time lag for changes in LPR issuances to take effect. This examination therefore anticipated the full effect of new legislation and subsequent fluctuations in approval levels by 2003-2004, following the same lag pattern indicated in 1998-

1999, the years after the 1996 implementation of major changes in federal immigration regulations.

REGIONAL DISPROPORTIONALITY AND VOLATILITY

Although all regions experienced declines in LPR approvals between 2002 and 2003, the most dramatic changes occurred in the North American, Asian, and European regions (See Figure 8.1).

Figure 8.1: Combined Regional LPR Approval Charts

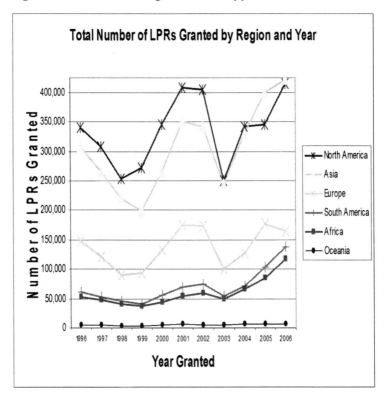

Among the top 3, the greatest decline in the period of study occurred in the North American region which had traditionally been the highest recipient of LPR approvals. After 2003, North America and Asia were almost even in the number of LPRs granted but by the beginning of 2004, and for the first time since 1996, Asia surpassed North America in the number of LPRs granted, exceeding the North American total by 54,560 approvals.

By 2006, the Asia region still had the highest number of approvals however; the gap between North American totals had significantly closed, only slightly exceeding the totals by just over 8,000 LPRs. Other significant changes occurred over the last two years of the period of study, in Africa, South America substantially exceed pre-9/11 totals while Europe hovered near the 9/11 totals and experienced a slight downward trend by 2006. Given the results of the document analysis, it was anticipated that the Asian region (which includes the majority of immigrant groups associated with Middle Eastern countries) would experience a sustained and comparatively disproportionate decline in LPR approvals after 9/11 due to the "folk devil" label elucidated by the media and in accordance with the hostility indicator. However, after the initial declines in 2003, LPR issuances in the Asian region actually experienced the highest approval levels throughout the 10-year span at the end of the period of study, even exceeding the North American totals, customarily the largest recipients of LPRs. Therefore, the disproportionality indicator was in fact implied by the rapid and substantial decline in all regional approvals by 2003, similar to the pattern exhibited in the pre-9/11 period but also ended the period of study with record high approvals in all categories, except Europe.

Correspondingly, some level of volatility was experienced in all regions in varying degrees between 2002 and 2006. In observing the fluctuation and subsequent restoration to pre-9/11 levels in most regions by the end of the period of study, variations were especially noted in the North American, European, and Asian regions. With a similar trend of issuances observed in all regions, it is evident that the federal government's "folk devil" was not only the Asian region, but also the disproportionately in the North American and European regions between 2002 and 2003, presenting a more general and cross-regional criminalization of the majority and traditionally largest recipient LPR groups.

Additionally, the rapid but short lived fluctuations in LPR issuances in all regions, characteristic of the volatility indicator during moral panics, were also evident during the post-9/11 period of study. By the end of the period of study, all regions except Europe had in fact exceeded their pre-9/11 levels, perhaps indicating a decreasing trend or even signifying an end of the moral panic against immigration.

TRUSTED FAMILY MEMBERS

Within the 5 chosen LPR categories, some dramatic changes were noted, mirroring many of the fluctuations that occurred within the regional LPR groupings (See Figure 8.2). Again, sudden and substantial declines in approvals granted were indicated between 2002 and 2003 in several categories, thus indicating both the disproportionality and volatility indicators within the LPR categories, and further signifying a moral panic environment.

Traditionally, the category receiving the greatest number of LPR approvals was "Immediate Relatives of U.S. Citizens". Beginning in 1999, the approval levels for this category were on a steady incline and finally peaked with a regionally combined total of over 480,000 approvals in 2002. By the end of the period of study, the category reached record high approvals, far exceeding the previous 2002 peak and achieving nearly 600,000 approvals. At the same time, The Refugee and Asylee and Employment Based categories were on pace to reach record peaks until 2005.

Figure 8.2 indicates the Refugee and Asylee category's continued to increase while the Employment based category suddenly plunged, dropping by over 87,000 approvals between 2005 and 2006, to low levels not occurring since before the new

9/11 regulations. Again, volatility is apparent by the record high numbers of family members approved for LPR status, in both family based categories (i.e. Immediate Relatives of U.S. citizens and Family Sponsored preferences) and the declining LPR approvals for immigrant groups in the Employment Based category, perhaps indicating a preference for immigrants with some family ties to the U.S., rather than those seeking employment and without any other obvious ties to the U.S.

Figure 8.2: Combined Regional LPR Approvals by Category

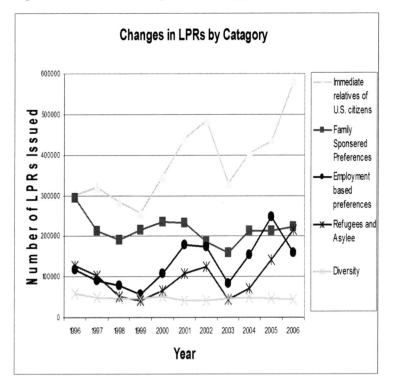

Utilizing the disproportionality indicator, it was also anticipated that a determination of a category of LPRs most effected after 9/11 would be evident, signifying an exaggerated threat from a particular category. The declining trend in approvals of employment based preferences may be a result of the fact that the applicant often has no familial ties to the U.S. upon application and that employment is typically the sole purpose this particular group of immigrants chooses to pursue LPR status. Large decreases in approvals by category typify the moral panic volatility indicator by signifying lingering social controls placed on specific LPR categories, in this case perhaps due to disproportionate concern or hostility against distinct immigrant groups or types of immigrants.

It is therefore possible that there was a shift in the perception of "trustworthiness" or decision to grant more LPR approvals to the applicants with existing family ties, rather than those simply seeking employment opportunities and without a family link. Volatility was therefore evident in two LPR categories where immigrants that already have established family connections to U.S. citizens, namely Immediate Relatives of U.S. citizens and Family Sponsored Preferences applicants, have gained continual increases in approvals since 2004; while at the same time, potential foreign employees seeking LPRs experienced a substantial downturn beginning in 2005.

In the pre-9/11 time period, the Family Sponsored Preferences category LPR approval level reached a low of 191,356 in 1998 then experienced only subtle changes until the post-9/11 period of study. The sharpest decline in this category was in the North American region falling dramatically between 2001 and 2003, experiencing a 44.1% decrease in just 2 years (See Figure 8.3). The only other region that experienced a significant decline over the same time period was Asia, an overall decrease of 16.2% over the same 2 year span. As noted in Figure 8.3, in both the 1998 and 2003 once the panic period subsided, most regions returned to their original levels of approval except the North American region which both times, has never recovered from the implementation of new federal regulations and even by the end of the period of study, had still not reached its pre-9/11 levels.

Figure 8.3: Family Sponsored Preference Category

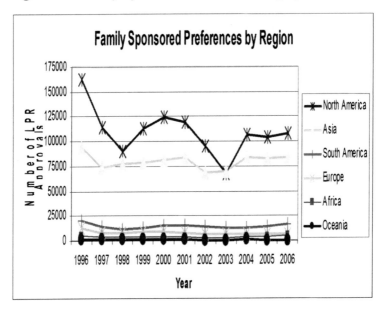

REGIONAL DISPARITY AND VARIATION

In the Employment Based Preference category, all areas experienced major fluctuations before returning to pre-9/11 figures but the Asian region exhibited the most drastic changes throughout the period of study. Again, the 2002 to 2003 years in this category indicated a sharp decrease in LPR Employment Based approvals of 51.7% in just 1 year (See Figure 8.4). By the end of the period of study, the Asian region reached a new high point, an increase of 153.9% over the 2004/2005 two year span but quickly fell again between 2005 and 2006. The 5 other regions also experienced a more than 50% drop in Employment Based Preference LPR approvals between 2002 and 2003, but in all cases each region exceeded the pre-9/11 levels by 2005, then began to return to pre-9/11 levels by 2006.

Figure 8.4: Employment Based Category

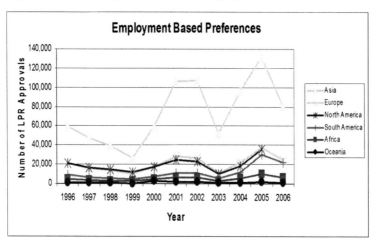

Figure 8.5: Diversity Category

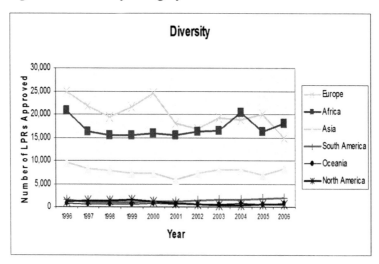

The sudden and dramatic fluctuation in the Employment Based Preferences category typifies the volatility indicator as the reasonably short panic episode subsided, and conditions returned to the pre-panic levels. Given that the Asian category had the most severe and erratic fluctuations, it may again be evident that the group was, by the end of the period of study, singled out for additional scrutiny as was anticipated due to the *folk devil* qualities of the Middle Eastern sub groupings within the Asian category.

In the Diversity category, LPR approvals began decreasing in 2000, before 9/11, in all geographical regions. Although the time period between 2002 and 2003 had the greatest effect in the other major LPR categories, the Diversity LPR approval levels remained relatively unaffected by the 9/11 attacks in 2001 (See Figure 8.5), indicating only slight changes by 2006, when compared to 2001 trends and totals. Finally, the Refugee and Asylee Adjustment LPR category experienced the greatest decline between 2002 and 2003 of all the regions and LPR categories during the period of study (See Figure 8.6).

Figure 8.6: Refugee and Asylee Adjustment Category

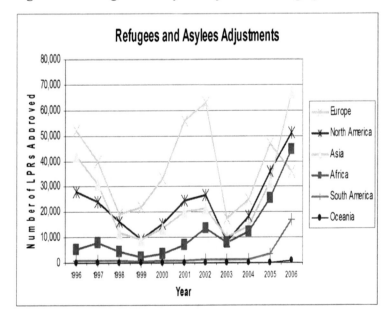

Overall the Refugee and Asylee Adjustment approvals experienced a 64.3% decrease in the combined regions, where the largest decrease was 72%, indicated in the European region. Three other regions also experienced significant declines in Refugee and Asylee LPR approval levels: North America with a 68.5% decrease, Asia with a 53.8% decrease, Africa with a 42.6% decrease, and Oceania with a 45.5% decrease. The South American region was the only area that experienced an increase in the Refugee and Asylee LPR approval levels with 24.2% between the 2002 and 2003. Beginning in 2003, all regions then experienced a dramatic rise in LPR approvals until the end of the period of study, substantially exceeding previous peak levels in the period of study in all regions except in Europe.

Given the individual LPR categories by region, it is evident that North America has experienced the most dramatic changes in the family sponsored categories where LPRs granted had not been restored to the pre-9/11 levels by the end of the period of study, as was the case in all the other regions. Europe experienced a similar fate in the Refugee and Asylee Adjustment category and was the only region that did not return to the pre-9/11 LPR approval levels in that category and in fact, by 2006, approvals were again on the decline. On the other hand, Asia has faced the most dramatic decline in the Employment Based category and had actually exceeded the pre-9/11 totals for a brief period but ultimately began sharply declining by 2006.

INDICATORS OF PANIC: FUELING THE ANXIETY

In this analysis, the federal immigration statistical comparison between pre and post-9/11 LPR issuances was used to determine the presence of the volatility and disproportionality moral panic indicators in post-9/11. As one of the characteristics of a moral panic environment, the sudden and wide fluctuations in the number and type of approvals in various LPR categories, coupled with the lingering LPR issuing changes, are both strong indications of the volatility indicator. These fluctuations were experienced in several notable categories; indicating some level of governmental apprehension against specific groups of immigrants after the September 11th attacks. The increased concern for particular immigrant groups mirrored the volatility trends that were exhibited in the pre-9/11 moral panicked era that took place shortly after the 1996 changes in federal regulations, also affecting the number of LPR issuances. However, despite the similarities with the 1996 trends, in LPR categories and issuances, the specific *folk devil* groups that were targeted by the federal government in the post-9/11 era had changed significantly in the types and regions where LPRs are issued.

With regard to the disproportionality indicator, it was anticipated that the federal government LPR issuances would change in the number of LPRs issued by region, specifically to countries in the Middle Eastern regions. Although disproportionality was evident in federal LPR approvals, instead of the expected changes in issuances within the regions traditionally associated with the Middle Eastern terrorist groups that were implicated in the 9/11 attacks, changes occurred in other groups that did not include the Middle Eastern countries associated with the 9/11 acts of terrorism. Therefore, in this study both moral panic indicators were indeed present and manifested however, the specific groups and regions that were targeted by the federal government through the LPR issuances were to some extent, unanticipated.

Identifying Specific Folk Devils

During the post-9/11 moral panic, volatility was denoted regionally with the targeting of particular LPR seeking groups as potential *folk devils* for varying periods of time, at the federal level. This reaction was anticipated as the post-9/11 federal government's act of scapegoating immigrants and consequently excluding them from specific LPR groups mirrored a common panic reaction which is, "particularly evident during moments of social crisis" (Welch 2006: 38) where moral panic conditions exist. In comparing the events of September 11th, analogous widespread reactions by the United States federal government against immigrants and immigration in general are not new phenomena. In fact, the practice of "rounding up immigrant groups during national security crises" is a repeating pattern in history (Guskin and Wilson 2007: 92). These reactions have historically occurred after events resembling 9/11, where rising concerns over both immigration and national security are perceptible; such as against the Japanese after WWII and after the Red Scare, which included periods beginning in WWI until 1920 and again during McCarthyism in the late 1940s to late 1950s (Guskin and Wilson 2007). In addition, the media and the public's response to immigrants and immigration in post-9/11 was anticipated, through the moral panic conditions indicated in this study, and both enhanced and supported by the federal government's *folk devil* crusade against immigrant LPR seeking groups.

The most interesting aspect of the LPR issuing trends occurring in post-9/11 were the changes in regions where the federal government granted LPR approvals, which were expected to be in the areas where specifically acknowledged *folk devils* resided. It was therefore anticipated that the Asian and African regions would experience the greatest declines or fluctuations in LPR approvals given that those two categories include all the countries identified and associated with Middle Eastern identity or the post-9/11 implicated *folk devils*. The greatest decline in LPR approvals however, occurred in the North American region, where historically, the highest numbers of LPRs had been granted and which is a region that does not include any of the Middle Eastern countries. Although this was the case, the volatility indicator was still evident in post-9/11 since it is not the actual categories or regions, or even the specific groups that fluctuate, that assist in substantiating a moral panic environment. It is only the fact that the characteristic abrupt, broad, and numerically measured fluctuations within the categories are apparent or evident during the panicked period. The volatility criterion for a post-9/11 moral panic was thus met by the observed large fluctuations, even as the approved Asian

LPR issuances actually increased, in one of the projected *folk devil* categories.

Welch (2006) asserted that: "Moral panic is indicative of turbulent societal reaction to social problems, particularly those producing a disaster mentality in which there is a widespread belief that society is endangered" (p. 100), again fueled by media and supported by the federal government and manifesting as the elusive disproportionality indicator. Accordingly, as one of the most difficult moral panic indicators to quantify, disproportionality stresses the excess of appropriate concern, measured empirically, and its relative proportionality to harm, along with observed changes over time. In this study, the changes in LPRs issued by region were in fact disproportionate to the level of harm that the North American region posed, given that none of the anticipated *folk devil* immigrant groups are typically associated with the region. Thus, in view of the participants involved in the 9/11 attacks, there is no compelling explanation for the specific increase in scrutiny towards the North American group in relation to its noticeably reduced number of post-9/11 LPR approvals. It may therefore be concluded that rather than targeting a specific group, a more general increase in scrutiny against immigrants occurred in a traditionally high LPR approval region; still generally indicating a high level of disproportionality.

On the other hand, given that the Asian population, that includes a large portion of the Middle Eastern countries listed under the federal categories, was the object of public and media scrutiny, the LPR approvals received favorable judgment by the U.S. government in that the LPR issuances increased rather than decreased. This result was counter to the assumption that the federal government would in fact reduce the number of LPRs approved in both the Asian and African regions, as the entire Middle Eastern population is included within those two federal categories. Also, given the hostility that was evident in the media and public's opinions, it was anticipated that the LPRs would be reduced in those two regions. Similarly, the increased number of number of Asian LPRs granted was disproportionate to the level that was expected to be issued to the category given its composition of many of the *folk devil* groups. Although this was the case, the disproportionality indicator was still evident by the numerical increase in LPR issuances in the Asian region and the sudden decrease in LPR in the North American region; resulting in an overall fluctuation in the issuance of LPRs at least in two categories. Further, without an initial or greater degree of threat from the North American region, disproportionality is also indicated empirically through that region's LPR issuance fluctuation alone.

In this analysis, three methods were used to examine the moral panic against immigrants, utilizing the indicators of concern, hostility, consensus, disproportionality, and volatility as exhibited in the post-9/11 era. These data indicate an increased proliferation in publishing of articles that associated immigrants with criminality by the media, a strong decrease in support for immigration by the public, and an increase in control over particular regions and LPR categories by the federal government. The next chapter will address the elements of each moral panic indicator, linking the results from the document analysis, poll data, and examination of federal immigration statistics with the corresponding indicator(s) as each was revealed.

CHAPTER 9

Terror of Immigration and War on Immigrants

When investigating the moral panic conception, the most important tasks are to establish: "What characterizes the moral panic? [and] How do we know when a moral panic takes hold on a given society?" (Goode and Ben-Yehuda, 1994: 33). It is these questions that must necessarily be addressed through specific indicators, by means of appropriate measures that determine the sudden and unpredictable nature of a moral panic environment. Based on the moral panic model and theoretical concepts of social control and deviance, the three analyses utilized in this study examined each indicator individually, then used a combined approach to seek out the succinct symptoms, illuminating post-9/11 moral panic conditions where immigrants in general have been criminalized by the media, public, and federal government and particular immigrant groups were clearly defined as *folk devils*. It is evident from the results of this study that after September 11th 2001, each moral panic indicator was manifested at varying degrees and several have continued to linger in U.S. society.

CONCERN

Since 9/11 and the inception of the PATRIOT Act, the issue of immigration in the U.S. has been constructed as a social problem where immigrants are routinely associated with a variety of social dangers including crime, terrorism, and national security in the media. Although the media are not the sole actors in constructing social problems, the media do "play a pivotal and strong role in defining and legitimizing the problem as well as promoting official interventions, policies, and programs" (Altheide 2002:146). Therefore, the media are an effective form of informal social control that is imperative to the proliferation of a moral panic and instrumental in distinguishing the subject of concern during a panic.

After the 9/11 terrorist attacks, the media's campaign against immigrants was evident as it began almost immediately with focused reporting on immigrants as related to a variety of criminal activities, thus aiding the increase in public fear and anxiety against them. As Welch (2006) asserts the overall effect of this type of reporting results in:

> Framing the issue in that manner reflects and reinforces not only public fear of terrorism, but also an undifferentiated social anxiety over national security, economic woes, crime, racial/ethnic minorities, immigrants, and foreigners. Those tensions compound the need to assign blame even if it means falsely accusing innocent persons for terrorism along with a host of other social problems. (p. 35)

This analysis discovered that there was in fact a comprehensive increase in the post-9/11 levels of reporting making the association between immigrants and criminality. These increases were discernible as a heightened anxiety over immigration that was prevalent in the media throughout the country; illuminating the concern indicator as a measurable and verifiable condition required to discern panicked condition (Welch 2002; Cohen 1972; Goode and Be-Yehuda 1994). The results showed increases in both the number of relevant articles and negative articles published, and even revealed an increase in the reporting of an individual's ethnicity or country of origin when reporting criminal activities; even in cases where the articles that had an entirely different focus and an individual's ethnic origin was immaterial.

Media Concern

By naming particular groups or adding foreign descents or ethnicities to U.S. citizens involved in crime or articles with an unrelated focus, the media effectively increased the coverage of immigrants as related to criminality within its publications; thus perhaps criminalizing immigrants and also those of foreign descent. One common tactic in reporting after 9/11 was the addition of a subject's ethnicity or descent in articles recounting criminal activities, even as the article's focus was not immigration or if the subject associated with crime was not necessarily foreign born but in many cases was in fact a U.S. citizen. Although the reference to a foreign descent did not enhance or further clarify the subject's motivation for engaging in criminal activity, the mere mention potentially criminalizes the immigrant group when it is included for no immediately obvious or apparent reason.

This method of informal social control suggests identifies foreign born groups are *folk devils* and further may provide the public with a target of hostility or "scapegoat". In an informal social control role, the media uses "scapegoating [which] by its very nature targets 'the other', a person or group that is perceived as being not only different from 'us' but potentially threatening to 'our' society. Especially when the 'the other' is different in terms of race, ethnicity, and religion" (Welch 2006: 71). Therefore, even in cases where criminal activities may have been perpetrated by U.S. citizens, the addition of an ethnic or foreign descent label further defined the subject as an "other" or outsider, needlessly suggesting a potential threat or need for increased suspicion against the immigrant groups referenced.

In the media analysis, there were many examples of articles where adding or implicating a foreign born descent seemed gratuitous. For instance, one article reporting a theft from a research lab in California described that the accused as "a naturalized citizen of Chinese descent" but did not elaborate on why the detail was relevant to the arrest or explore the issue further, it simply implied that as the accused is foreign born, he does not really belong to U.S. society and was in effect, although a citizen, clearly identified as an being an 'other'.

In another article, there was a report of an investigation into an identity theft crime where "an American born woman and an Israeli man" were accused; the article later clarifies the female suspect's ethnicity further by indicating that the American was of Russian descent, again a seemingly irrelevant but pejorative detail. In articles where immigration was not the primary issue and need not have been included in the reports, the criminal association of immigrants was still included, for example:

> Trailed early Thursday by news cameras, state game wardens arrested Mark Golmyan, 54, owner of the Gastronom Russian Deli on Geary Street, along with four other San Francisco residents accused of buying the caviar for up to $140 a pound and then selling it to Bay Area residents, mostly of Russian descent. ("Sturgeon Poaching Leads to Caviar Sting", The *Associated Press State & Local Wire*, May 5, 2005)

The article therefore, implicates the immigrant group as being involved in criminal activity even though the report was simply relaying an incident of sturgeon poaching and subsequent arrest of a deli owner.

Another example of the kinds of reporting that included ethnicity or named and immigrant group where there was no further enhancement to the story, except to implicate the criminal association to a particular immigrant group, was:

> A doctor arrested and charged with illegally providing prescription drugs to addicts has been freed on $2,500 bail. Prosecutors argued that Dr. Sarfraz A. Mirza, who is of Pakistani descent, is a flight risk and that his bail

should be consistent with those charged with serious drug offenses. Brevard County Judge George Turner disagreed. We argued for higher bond because these are serious offenses," Assistant State Attorney Wayne Holmes told The Orlando Sentinel for its Thursday editions. "In our view, it's no different than cocaine or other illegal substances harming our community. ("Brevard County Doctor Freed After Prescription Drug Arrest", *The Associated Press State & Local Wire*, July 30, 2003)

In this article, no further details were presented therefore the casual reader's assumption is that given the foreign descent of the accused, there is an inherent suspicion that the subject may be considered a flight risk although the article did not indicate if the subject was a U.S. citizen or native born, instead the assumption of criminality rests entirely with the fact that the subject is of foreign descent.

Concern was also evident among the public as the heightened level of anxiety was directed at specific immigrant groups, determined by an increase in the number of reported hate crimes. Although these articles were not accusing the immigrants of committing criminal acts, the association between immigrants and criminality and the frequency of hate crime occurrences both suggest an overall heightened anxiety against particular immigrant populations in society. In fact, the sharp increase in the number of hate crimes occurring against Asian groups and especially Middle Eastern groups, further illustrates the notion of labeling or "othering", where specific immigrant groups were targeted for attacks as a means to protect the public from the perceived threat of outsiders (Welch 2006). These tactics were especially common after 9/11 and often directed toward Muslim/Arab Americans where a variety of forms of harassment or assault, acts of vandalism, and instances of boycotting were frequently reported (Mukherjee 2003). It is evident from this study that after September 11 and throughout the U.S., "the dynamic of 'othering' abounds...[the attacks] serve to sharpen an otherwise vague notion of 'them'...they have quickly emerged as the 'usual suspects' eligible for suspicion, blame, and persecution" (Welch 2006: 73).

Public Concern

In a moral panic environment, hate crime proliferates as concern over a particular group is amplified by the media, as a form of informal social control (Welch 2006; Cohen 1985). The media messages are subsequently responded to by the public and then manifest as the public labels or identifies particular groups as threatening and valid targets of hostility (Becker 1963). With the well documented wave of hate crimes that occurred after September 11th, the media reports provided persistent examples of the presence of the concern indicator among the public against particular immigrant groups.

As the concern indicator was proliferated in media reporting, concern among the general public was further evidenced in the post-9/11 public opinion poll results. Poll participants continually indicated immigration as an important domestic problem and the poll trends suggested that it was becoming more of a problem than the other typically related issues of national security and terrorism. With the assistance from the media in making increased associations of immigrants engaging in criminal activities, changes in the perception of immigrants among the public were noted and as expected in a moral panic environment, infers a higher level of suspicion toward particular groups in society and the groups' impact on society (Rothe and Muzzatti 2004; Slone and Shoshani 2010).

Although the number of respondents in support of a decrease in immigration peaked immediately following 9/11 and had never reached the height of pre-9/11 levels, since 9/11 there has been an overall increase in support for maintaining present levels and a corresponding decline the respondents indicating support of an increase in immigration which greatly fluctuated near the end of the period of study. The last poll considered in this study fluctuated in its sentiment toward immigration as a "good or bad thing". Although the evidence was not as strong as in the other poll results, the poll taken in 2005 displayed a sudden and abrupt drop in respondents' "good thing" reactions, typifying the episodic, heightened anxiety of the concern indicator.

This analysis focused on three polls however, other public opinion research conducted since September 11th (*See* Cainkar 2004, Kettl 2004, McLean 2004, Parenti 2002, Welch 2002, and Welch 2006) supports the assertion that public sentiment with regard to immigration had been generally negative and especially accusatory towards Arab and Middle Eastern groups since the attacks. In this study, there was evidence of a successful campaign by the media and followed by the public, which clearly defined several immigrant groups as *folk devils* thus criminalizing these immigrants and making them the object of concern in the post-9/11 panicked society. Finally, as perhaps the most influential source in shaping public opinions and attitudes about crime and crime victims (Chermak 2004), the news media's informal controls are enhanced by the government, the primary formal social control group, through policy support and by providing legitimacy to the panic against immigrants, resulting in the preservation of political, economic, and social goals (Paletz and Entman 1981).

Governmental Concern

The concern indicator was evident by the federal government's heightened anxiety which denoted by the comparative reduction in the number of regionally issued LPRs between 2002 and 2003 and the decline in issuances in four of the five LPR categories during the same period. As observed in the 1996 federal legislation changes affecting immigration and LPR issuances, changes resulting from the PATRIOT Act did not fully materialize immediately but were certainly palpable by the 2002-2003 period. Also targeting immigrants as potential threats to security, lower levels of government including state and local agencies displayed heightened anxiety and provided support to federal efforts by furthering the goals of formal social control at a the regional or community levels.

Although the federal government's response to 9/11 was a general "crusade against terror" (Welch 2006: 64), on a more localized level, government agencies responded to the 9/11 attacks by questioning foreign born residents as a means of reducing potential threats and heightening public safety, again implying threats from specific foreign residents in the community. In Maine, for example, "local and federal agencies have interviewed dozens, if not hundreds, of foreign-born Maine residents. Most of those from northern Africa, the Middle East and South Asia" (*The Associated Press State & Local Wire* 2001). Even two years after 9/11, continued increased vigils targeting immigrants were common but cast more of a general and ambiguous suspicion and against groups as was the case where "agents in Oklahoma have been keeping an eye on suspicious individuals doing suspicious things, including those of Middle Eastern descent who may be conducting unusual financial transactions" (*The Associated Press State & Local Wire* 2003). It is these types of generalized concerns and continual ambiguous vigils that typify the concern indicator in a moral panic environment.

With all the common moral panic participants or claims makers involved, it is apparent that concern indicator unfolded immediately after the attacks in 2001 and continued to linger throughout the post-9/11 five-year time span. With an immediate increase in articles relating immigrants to criminality, concern was initiated by the media in September 2001 and continued vacillating, but elevated, until the end of the period of study. The media reaction coincided with the implementation of the PATRIOT Act in 2001 however; it was not until the 2002 and 2003 period when new federal legislation exhibited its full effect, and among other changes, a consequential and terse decline in LPRs issuances found in this study. Finally, the public's anxiety in general began immediately after 9/11 with the reported frequency of hate crimes, continued with an overall "bad" public opinion of immigration, and has lingered with a steady increase in the public's sentiment that immigration is an ongoing, principal problem in the U.S.

HOSTILITY

With the concern indicator revealed, it follows that the media, public, and federal government's heightened anxiety must next be directed at a target of apprehension, represented by a specific "folk devil" in moral panic terms. The essence of the hostility indicator then may be measured as an increase in both formal and informal controls are directed at a particular group, as was elucidated by the concern indicator. From the results of this investigation there was a definite labeling of immigrant groups that materialized in both general and specific manifestations and as increased levels of formal and informal controls.

Targeted Informal Controls

Given the increases in hate crimes directed at immigrant groups and in the reporting of immigrants associated with criminality, "The fact that the terrorists of 9/11 were not US citizens...seemed to justify a certain 'state of general suspicion' (of being a terrorist) against all foreigners, but particularly against those who shared a common Arab origin with those terrorists" (Saux 2007: 58). This is the fundamental nature of hostility in a moral panic environment as heightened informal social controls imposed upon immigrants were indeed evident along with an immediate and obvious increase in the post-9/11 period that named Asian groups, especially Middle Eastern ethnicities and descendants, as targets of hostility. Several polls that were conducted during the period of study also indicated an increased focus on terrorism and national security as the primary cause of the attacks, blaming immigration controls as the main area of concern (Adelman 2004) and more specifically targeting the Middle Eastern/Arab population as the primary target of concern (Cainkar 2004).

Therefore, although media attention to the generic "foreign born/descent" reference remained high throughout the period of study, in post-9/11 articles the greatest increases in references were clearly made in the Middle Eastern immigrant groups, making them the most well defined and apparent *folk devils* in media reporting. The Middle Eastern group was also the most frequently targeted victim of the publics' heightened anxiety, in the form of hate crimes, exceeding the second most victimized group by 168.3%. Another conspicuous development in the post-9/11 reporting within the immigrant references was discovered. In addition to the top referenced general "Middle Eastern" category, more particularized groups were also recognized, including broader geographical mentions and added Middle Eastern ethnicities referenced; thus expanding the overall number of immigrants in the population that the media associated with criminality and "attracting greater scrutiny to otherwise undifferentiated 'Middle Easterners'" (Welch 2006: 73).

Targeted Formal Controls

As the primary agency, responsible for implementing formal social controls, the federal government's responses to terrorist threats or similar devastating events in U.S. history have been well documented. Similar to the crisis controls implemented during the suspension of habeas corpus after the civil war, the Palmer Raids of WWI, and the Japanese Internment of WWII (Chang 2002; Gerstle 2004; Zinn 2002), the PATRIOT Act legislation responded to 9/11 with similar sweeping legislation, clearly targeting immigrants as a primary source of trepidation in society. The extent of the new federal powers are unprecedented and also somewhat ambiguous, in that the new laws permitted nearly all of the current 20 million U.S. immigrants to be subjected to military tribunals, increased surveillance, expedited deportation, and indefinite detention (Zinn 2002).

Further, PATRIOT Act legislation targets immigrants especially in its ability to question and detain noncitizens without even a criminal conviction for an extended period of time if attorney general "certifies" that there are "reasonable grounds to believe" that they are somehow connected to terrorist activities and release would likely threaten national security (Chang 2002, Kuzma 2004). Therefore, not only did the PATRIOT Act allow the imposition of a variety of general restrictions and controls on immigrants but also it specifically targeted Middle Eastern groups by rounding up and detaining more than 1,200 immigrants within two months of 9/11, deeming them as suspicious, for questioning and indefinite detention (Welch 2002). Already subjected to informal controls, it is evident that with the implementation of these types of sweeping formal social controls, "Immigrants and asylum-seekers are perfect candidates to be considered 'folk devils' in the context of counter-terrorism policy" (Saux 2007: 63).

Increased governmental formal controls were most evident in this study's results as overall declines in LPR issuances over the period of study were evident in all regions. Although these declines affected virtually all immigrant groups, the decreases were particularly noted in the North American and Asian regions and in the latter region, were very pronounced in the Employment Based category, historically the highest LPR beneficiaries. It is the immigrants seeking LPR status only for employment purposes that do not usually have familial ties or necessarily any additional connections to the U.S. and therefore; the candidates may be seen as the LPR group that garners the most suspicion in the application process, in view of all the LPR categories. Given the many applicant classifications, also noted was also a more general, overall decline in LPR issuances that was evident across all categories.

Similar to the federal government's response to drug users in the "war on drugs" and given the wholesale radical declines in LPR issuances between 2002 and 2003, the new PATRIOT Act regulations have effectively erased all defining lines that identified particular groups of immigrants as potentially threatening, instead criminalizing all immigrant groups seeking

LPR approvals in the post-9/11 period. This all inclusive response was however anticipated as:

> [B]eing that law precepts have necessarily a general nature and given that a distinction between foreigners (Arabs and not-Arabs) would certainly not be in accordance with the rule of law and would not respect the principle of equality, all foreigners were put at a disadvantage, irrespective of their origin. (Saux 2007: 58)

Essentially, as the federal effort was aimed at national security, reducing terrorism, and protection against *folk devils* targeted formal control have breached their boundaries in this pursuit when it comes to identifying particular immigrant groups as targets of suspicion; it has started "pushing the pendulum from care to control" (Lyon 2003: 11).

CONSENSUS

The consensus indicator is characterized by widespread agreement that a particular group is considered suspect and potentially threatening to society. Consequently, during a moral panic, some resistance or opposition to the purported menace must occur. As discovered in the document analyses, increases in post-9/11 negative articles and media references to foreign born groups associated with criminal activity were evident in all regions of the country, elucidating an extensive concurrence among media publications in reporting immigrants, potentially as likely and frequent sources of peril.

Similar to the concern and hostility indicator outcomes, the increase in poll respondents' anxiety over immigration and in the number of hate crimes reported in all regions gives the indication that the public's response to immigrants was observable throughout the country as a response to the corresponding perceived threat from the foreign born population.

Public Consensus

Thompson (1998) asserts that publicly perceived social problems do not suddenly materialize in the moral panic environment. Essentially, societal conditions beset with anxiety must first exist and be equipped with a receptive or risk-conscious public which is open to the media and government's agitation of particular social problems (Thompson 1998: 29). As is the case since 9/11, issues of immigration, national security, and terrorism have been habitually linked (Aldeman 2004) and have provided a social context for responding to perceived societal threats, garnering much of the media's attention and necessitating formal solutions, in the form of government action (Cainkar 2004; Zucconi 2004). It is under these conditions that opinion polls revealed a moral panic against immigrants across the country, given government's response to the "war on terror", by the implementation of the PATRIOT Act, and the post-9/11 social environment that existed, fueled by the media, the public was highly susceptible to hostility against immigrants.

Although not as explicit as public opinion toward terrorism and national security, the fact that immigration was indicated as one of the most important problems for almost every poll in the post-9/11 period of study, and so infrequently in the pre-9/11 data, indicates a clear and increased public perception of the potential threat that immigrants pose. This indication was also observable in the changes to respondents support for a "decrease" or maintenance of "present levels" of immigration when compared to those in support of an "increase" in levels. This illustration does not suggest that all of society was engulfed in the panic as the element of consensus in a moral panic does not require that the whole society is in fact consumed (Cohen 1985; Goode and Ben Yehuda 1994). Instead, it must be established that at least a fairly widespread segment of the population (Goode and Ben-Yehuda 1994) is engaged in some amount of public disquiet which agrees that "where social control has disappeared, it must be put back in place" (Baerveldt et al. 1998: 36).

Federal Consensus

In observing the historical practice of responding to terrorism, federal crime and social controls are frequently prone to the expansion of criminal laws and criminalization of targeted and ostensibly threatening populations (Saux 2007). In fact, over the last few centuries, U.S. immigration policy has been based on directing restrictions towards groups that threaten national security, and at different times, "permitting exclusion, deportation, detention, or heightened scrutiny" (Engle 2004: 64) to targeted groups, when applicable.

The federal response to 9/11 was therefore predictable as "political actors in...America have repeatedly chosen to respond to widespread public concern about crime and security by formulating policies that punish and exclude" (Garland 2001: 202), an especially important task in response to immigration policy where federal institutions are responsible for both the protection of the country from terrorists and foreign threats and balancing the "positive benefits which immigration has and continues to provide" to U.S. society (Lebowitz and Podheiser 2002). The PATRIOT Act implementations with regard to immigration therefore have addressed the issues of terrorism however; it appears that the residual effect has also punished particular categories of immigrants that have historically enjoyed favorable and long-established admission.

With regard to LPR approvals, this examination found that all regions have not continued to experience decreases that were indicated in the 2002-2003 period. However both Europe and North America, traditionally large LPR recipients, have not yet been restored to their pre-9/11 levels. By LPR category, these data indicate that while the "Immediate Relatives of U.S. Citizens" category, where immigrants already have some close family ties to the U.S., has experienced substantial increases.

Conversely, the Employment Based approvals, the LPRs with the most rigorous background checks and scrutiny of qualifications, using a complex labor certification process and employability, skill, and advanced education requirements (Ting

2003) are in fact on the decline. Again, although new PATRIOT Act policies are targeted at reducing terrorism and security threats, the LPR declines clearly indicate a shift in time-honored confidence that scrutinized LPR immigrants have come to depend on, casting a new suspicion on LPR groups that have historically earned much confidence from the U.S. immigration system, both by region and application category.

DISPROPORTIONALITY

Although the disproportionality indicator may be observed and measured using a variety of methods (Goode and Ben-Yehuda 1994), previous moral panic studies suggest that disproportionality is often the most elusive and difficult to determine (Baerveldt et al., 1998; Waddington 1986). Goode and Ben-Yehuda (1994) assert that the measure must be empirical in nature and some indication that public concerns exceed the relative level of genuine hazards or tangible threats posed. Therefore, as was selected for this study, examining the developing concern over the problem through a historical comparison would yield the most dependable measure (Baerveldt et al. 1998) of disproportional moral panic conditions.

From the results of the regional document analyses, indicating an increase in overall reporting relating immigrants with criminality, perceived threats that immigrants posed did not correspond with specific events occurring in U.S. society, such as additional major terrorist attacks, which customarily increase anxiety over immigration or would imply comparative dangers from immigrants that are directed specifically towards U.S. society. Rather, it was found that "social anxieties instigated either at decision/opinion-making levels or in localized settings by the general public can be and [were] spread by national and local media" (Pijpers 2006: 94).

Disproportionality was also evident from both the public and federal governments' perspective. After 9/11, poll respondents have consistently indicated immigration as one of the "most important problems" in varying degrees which equates to an overall comparative rise and strong indication that the issue is an undoubtedly more significant concern to the public on a continual basis, especially when compared to the pre-9/11 poll responses. The public's general preoccupation, continued anxiety, and enduring concern over immigration is seemingly unwarranted given that federal regulations have not changed significantly since the PATRIOT Act was implemented and since there are have not been any major terrorist attacks against the country, nor have there been any other major civil disturbances directly involving immigrants since 9/11 that would draw suspicion or garner additional scrutiny towards immigrant groups.

As noted from the consensus indicator, the federal response to the threat of immigrants was again conspicuous in the overall sharp decline in LPRs granted between 2002 and 2003 and some of the developing category trends since 9/11. Indicative of the overall changes to antiterrorist legislation and governmental strategies that have developed since 9/11, disproportionality was indicated as the target of new PATRIOT Act policies addressed immigration as a whole, rather than just targeting particular groups associated in the media or by the public as potential threats. Similarly, the volatility indicator was prevalent in all regions and across all included categories in varying degrees.

VOLATILITY

With all of the other moral panic conditions present, the volatility indicator aids in determining the length and measuring magnitude of the episode. Volatility is characterized as an oscillating disquiet over a particular issue that is observable among the media, public, and government, appearing in short and sudden episodes, then just as abruptly, dissipating for periods of time (Goode and Ben-Yehuda; Thompson 1998; Critcher 2003). Although the initial panic subsides, the volatility indicator is typified as the issues do not dissipate entirely but instead recur and may abruptly rise as sporadic episodes of panic occur. Essentially, as the distinct episodes of a panic may be brief and sporadic in nature, the fundamental issue that is the source of the panic remains as a more permanent and continuous focus (Critcher 2003; Baerveldt et al. 1998).

Intermittent Episodes

As this study considered the issue of immigration a 10-year span, using 9/11 as the midpoint, overall trends indicated that the episodic nature of moral panics was indicated several times over the post-9/11 period among the media, public, and federal government. Firstly, volatility was evident since 2001 in the media as sudden and sweeping negative reports of immigrants and articles relating immigrants to criminality began immediately after 9/11, which dissipated quickly, and then continued to erratically rise and fall over time. Secondly, as noted in the concern indicator, given the opinion polls that identified immigration as an important among a range of other social problems, both intermittently and continuously, meets the criterion for volatility. Finally, with the sharp changes in LPR issuances between 2002 and 2003, then equally as dramatic rises that followed, typifies the characteristic of volatility as displayed in the federal government's response to immigration in a moral panic environment.

Enduring Issues

Pijpers (2006) asserts that the episodic nature of a panic environment may be attributed to the introduction of new social problems that pose additional or greater threats, thus quelling the original panic, but allowing the broader issues to remain in focus. As non-citizens and foreign visitors are often associated with a host of other recurring social issues, such as legal versus illegal immigration, crime, national security, and terrorism, it is anticipated that over time the larger issue of immigration among the public, media, and government will therefore logically endure. Interestingly, previous moral panic research has entirely excluded elaborating on the presence of this indicator (Burns and

Crawford 1999) given that the nature of the fluctuations depicted by the volatility indicator are very similar to the characteristics found in the concern and disproportionality indicators however, it is the enduring, episodic panic against immigration that differs, making its inclusion in this study not only warranted but also indispensable.

With the media and public opinion over immigration showing sharp fluctuations in the post-9/11 era, support levels for immigration shifted suddenly and unpredictably, possibly in response to a variety of domestic occurrences involving immigrants or perhaps other social problems occurring abroad. At the same time the federal governments' abrupt increases and subsequent declines in the number of LPR issuances in a range of areas indicated an elevated level of anxiety which manifested as volatility against immigrants since 9/11. These episodes fluctuated unpredictably; similar to the action observed both the concern and disproportionality indicators.

The next and last chapter will conclude this investigation with a discussion of the outcome of the application of the moral panic conception to immigration in the post-9/11 U.S. society, prospects, and implications for future studies.

CHAPTER 10
The Immigration Impasse

It is evident that the media, public, and federal government provoked and sustained a moral panic environment against immigrants in U.S. society, which began during the "war on terror", shortly after the terrorist attacks on September 11th 2001. Through an examination of the five traditional moral panic indicators of concern, hostility, consensus, disproportionality, and volatility, the reaction of the three habitual panic participant groups had indeed manifested as a prolonged and comprehensive criminalization of immigration that includes a variety of immigrant groups, extending across all regions of the United States. The integrated theoretical approach used for this analysis therefore has arguably provided greater insights into how and why post-9/11 U.S. society became engrossed in a moral panic against immigration.

As outlined in Chapters 1 and 2 of this study, the inclusion of several theoretical models, that incorporated both formal and informal social control, deviance, and labeling, has clarified and assisted in explaining the distinct attributes found in the post-9/11 moral panic society. The panic was initially rooted in formal social controls employed in the "war on terror", which in this study's context, included the federal government's implementation of the PATRIOT Act, acting as a, "legislative/administrative process by which human actions [were] defined as criminal and those committing them subjected to social control." (Lemert and Winter 2000: 263). The formal execution of social controls ultimately effected, and continue to

143

affect, immigration in several key ways, including through the number of legal permanent residents gaining approval status, in all issuing categories.

At the same time, the supporting complementary informal means of social control, spawned by media reporting and public opinion concerns, caused a further labeling of *folk devils* in society which produced the subsequent criminalization of several specific groups within the immigrant population. With the formal and informal means of social control as complements and the post-9/11 socially constructed problem of immigration generated by the "war on terror", criminal or deviant immigrant groups in society were, in effect, openly labeled as targets of suspicion and cause for panic; a moral panic against immigration had thus been revealed.

SOCIAL CONTROL, DEVIANCE, AND LABELING THEORY

From the three sources of information utilized in this examination, the criminalization of immigration was observed at varying times in the post-9/11 period as society was engrossed in a panicked environment. The panic against immigrants was exhibited by three distinct means, materializing as a result of both formal and informal social controls imposed on specific groups in society, which were subsequently labeled as the deviant or *folk devil* population. Therefore, the findings from the current study have several implications for the moral panic conception, but also for social control, deviance, and labeling theories.

First observed in this study was the informal but widespread media amplification of the association of immigrants with implicit and latent dangers in society. These newly created dangers became social problems, observed through the continual bombardment of post-9/11 "war on terror" reporting that focused on reports of criminal activity, attributed to several, specific problem groups among the foreign-born population. The reporting effectively, but informally, criminalized immigrants by assigning deviant labels when making frequent associations between immigrants and various acts of criminality. Therefore, as observed through disproportionate media coverage of immigrants in post-9/11 reporting:

> [T]he construction of social problems, particularly crime problems, follow some fairly predictable themes and rhetorical patterns. These themes generate public support and attention and give crime problems a sustainable momentum. (Kappeler and Kappeler 2004: 177)

Hence, the momentum of the new socially constructed problem of a deviant immigrant population in post-9/11 reporting would eventually become especially evident and pervasive among the general public.

Amid such vast increases in the association of the foreign-born population with criminality in post-9/11 reporting, the media was informally able to determine, for a panicked, public populace, which groups should in fact be deemed and targeted as *folk devils*. As is the case in panicked conditions, "news events fuel coverage, but the media, through its editorial decisions, helps determine what issues are to be perceived as important by the public" (Lee 1998: 61). Thus, it was the success of the media's post-9/11 informal social controls that aided in convincing a panicked society who in fact should be targeted as *folk devils*; namely the foreign-born population and more specifically, the Middle Eastern/Arab population. As is exactly the case when imposing deviant labels in panicked conditions, Lemert and Winter (2000) suggested that:

> [D]eviance can be made explicit by saying that human beings and their actions may become objects or subjects of disapproval, condemnation, penalties, ostracism, banishment, segregation, treatment, and unsolicited help or even friendly advice – that is, of social controls. (p. 63)

The media therefore sustained its informal, but highly effective, criminalization of particular immigrant groups with the assistance of comparable government imposed formal social controls.

As perhaps the most effective means of social control, the government serves to formally label the *folk devils* in a moral panic environment. In this study, the comprehensive reduction in LPR approvals indicated a sweeping distrust of LPR seeking immigrants across all categories. Accordingly, the federal government with a post-9/11 "war on terror" mindset had formally applied the PATRIOT Act and imposed new formal restrictions on the immigrant population, a predictable approach as:

> Much of social control of terrorism pertains to the future – what might happen where - rather than to what has already occurred...it may entail special surveillance and travel restrictions for individuals socially similar to terrorists as well. (Black 2004: 15)

The result of such daunting social controls was an enhanced feeling of distrust against the targeted "folk devil" population; further excluding from or limiting access of these identified immigrant groups to mainstream society. With the formal identification of *folk devils*, the media's informal controls assisted in further separating the immigrant population by reducing the public's positive sentiment towards them, which in turn, negatively affected the level of confidence the public held in the prevailing U.S. immigration system.

Taken together, formal and informal social controls initiated by moral entrepreneurs are extremely effective in targeting a *folk-devil* population and leading the public in a moral panic. Given the "war on terror" post-9/11 panicked society against immigrants, the:

Process of situating terrorism within the cultural shock of previously constructed crime problems [like immigration after 9/11] makes the collective ideology more powerful and understandable. The media official alerts, in nightly news sound bites the media are a conduit for political rhetoric and the claims of law enforcement officials. (Kappeler and Kappeler 2004: 188)

Therefore, working in concert with the media, the widespread panic against all types of immigrants was in fact achieved. The panicked social climate thus validated the call for sweeping formal controls that were designed to isolate and monitor the immigrant population, at the expense of citizens' rights and in the name of national security; both justified under the guise of defending the "war on terror". In post-9/11 society then, "Terrorism has found a place in the public explanation for crime-reinforcing other previously constructed social problems" (Kappeler and Kappeler 2004: 188); namely, the "problem" of immigration and the criminalization of immigrants in U.S. society.

GUILTY BY ASSOCIATION

Given the moral panic model, the outcome of this investigation indicates that the implementation of federal legislation followed by the focused support from the media and growing public distrust resulted in not only a general criminalization of immigrants the post-9/11 society, but also a trend toward grouping all immigrants together in one generic suspect group. Hence, once the targeted *folk devils* were identified, they were publically subjected to both suspicion and mistrust by the media, government, and general public. Therefore, the criminalization of immigration in post-9/11 society was confirmed in typical and sequential moral panic fashion.

The implementation of new federal legislation like the PATRIOT Act, is the federal government's attempt to undo damage caused by momentous societal shifts, as had occurred after the 9/11 attacks. It is under this pretext that the federal government imposed:

> [E]xtensive new disciplines and controls, though it has been a feature of these developments that they have been targeted against particular social groups rather than universally imposed...a retrofitting of controls, an attempt to put the lid back on a newly disordered world. (Garland 2001: 195)

Cole (2003) suggested that the federal government's imposition of the PATRIOT Act as a response to the 9/11 attacks has in fact, failed in 3 principle areas. These failings have greatly contributed to and bolstered the moral panic environment. First, the federal government's actions in response to terrorism are an overreaction, replicating the McCarthy era's philosophy of guilt by association with regard to immigrants (Cole 2003) which consequently, and also erroneously, focuses suspicion on identity rather than conduct (Cole 2002). Second, also as a repetition of past governmental errors in overreaction, they have sacrificed some freedoms and equal treatment of immigrants which inadvertently has had parallel, similar restrictive effects on citizen's rights and liberties in the post-9/11 era. Finally, the PATRIOT Act has effectively traded a selected group of immigrants' liberties, namely Middle Eastern/Arab immigrants, for the security of the country (Cole 2003). Again, it is this type of government reaction that harkens back to the McCarthy era's time of shame and questionable tactics, which had proven no more effective on increasing national security then, with respect to immigrants, than today's PATRIOT Act.

As also indicated by the results of this analysis, all classes of immigrants have begun suffering from criminalization. This unfortunate and damaging outcome was spawned by the media, public, and even federal reactions to immigration that do not always clearly differentiate between the type of immigrant or status an immigrant holds in society. In fact, the term immigration implies a legal process of migrating to another country while "illegal immigration" is not, by definition, immigration at all; but rather, simply illegal migration. The immigrant reference therefore, frequently and erroneously includes both legal and illegal aliens in just one, demonized category. Thus, a check of the current state of media, public, and governmental responses to immigration reveals that "while policies and attitudes toward legal and illegal immigration are theoretically separable, from a practical standpoint, they are not" (Hood and Morris 1998: 12).

In the moral panic conception, sweeping categorizations are one of the great contributors to widespread panic that certainly helps explain the holistic demonizing or criminalization of *folk devils* that so often takes place during a panic episode. Although the results of this analysis found evidence of each moral panic indicator against immigration, there was an additional aspect of panic that erupted in post-9/11 that was not effectively or directly addressed by any of the five traditional indicators.

One More Indicator?

The exploration of moral panic conditions, using Goode and Ben-Yehuda's (1994) five indicators, is an effective means to observe socially constructed problems that gain prominence in the media, affect an extensive segment of the public, and require the attention and requisite official reaction of the government at various points in time. However, given the many available categories of aliens and current tendency to immediately criminalize all immigrants, by placing both legal and illegal in one category, an additional indicator suggested by Baerveldt, Bunkers, Winter, and Kooistra (1998) could provide further and more significant insight into the current moral panic against immigrants.

Baerveldt, Bunkers, Winter, and Kooistra (1998) suggested the notion of 'misdirectedness' as another important consideration in the moral panic environment in that, "the occurrence and dominance of misdirected standard reactions to a problem" (p. 42) are not sufficiently examined by the other existing indicators. Given the frequency of misdirected occurrences and their dominance found in a variety of issues related to immigration, it may be appropriate to explore the degree to which legal immigrants are being confused, misclassified, and thus criminalized, along with illegal migrants. Consequently, rather than adding an additional "misdirectedness" indicator, it may be more appropriate to expand the hostility indicator and include an exploration of misguided or misplaced hostility, further clarifying the true course and distinctive targets manifested in a moral panic. Either way, enhancing the understanding of the extent to which hostility is "misdirected" would certainly clarify the degree to which a panic is entrenched in society, (i.e. against specific or all types of immigrant groups) and may help verify the important delineation between hostility directed at legal immigration or illegal migration.

FUTURE CONSIDERATIONS

Future projects that embark upon a similar study might benefit from those approaches that were initially considered but not utilized. First, although the use of surveys was initially considered to complement poll statistical data, they have been purposely excluded for two reasons.

As the subject of this analysis includes the observation of media connections between immigrants and their levels of criminality, questioning participants about this issue would necessarily include the insinuation that immigrants do in fact engage in crime. This was not the purpose of the project and it would be difficult to question participants in a manner that does not clearly imply an existing criminal connection, without blatantly soliciting that kind of response. As the definition of criminality used here encompasses social control, it was determined that poll data would therefore better indicate several aspects that suggest criminality, without including an overt exclamation.

Another reason surveys were not conducted is that the questions used in most national polls have complete figures for the time frame that was examined in this study. Further, poll questions have been asked continuously, at regular intervals rather than only after potential "opinion changing" events, such as terrorist attacks on other countries, which assists in illuminating trends that have developed over the span of time in question. The uninfluenced, trend identifying benefit of poll data was the primary reason for the selection of existing poll data although additional polls that were excluded from this study should be considered in future research as they may complement and possibly further illuminate the public's sentiment on related immigration issues.

The second method that was cautiously considered for this study was the document analysis. With the selection of a document analysis, the time frame chosen for this study found evidence that frequent media references and focused reporting have induced moral panics against a particular population of immigrants, namely Middle Eastern groups. The notion of criminalization as an attribute of moral panics is therefore supported. However, although the extent to which U.S. society is experiencing a moral panic was explored on a limited basis in this study, it should be explored further in a future study using additional and perhaps expanded research terms, other forms of media, to include television and even radio transmissions, and additional time periods, to observe changes as new federal immigration policies and legislation are imposed.

As with poll data, the choice of federal immigration statistics for the study period provided a sufficient span to observe changes in the number of immigrants that were affected since the inception of the PATRIOT Act and other post-9/11 federal regulations affecting immigration. Although it is difficult to predict the exact length of time needed to observe all the changes to federal LPR approval rates, the trend data in the pre and post time frames allowed an opportunity to examine a scenario similar to the changes that were imposed in the 1996 immigration laws and implementation of contemporary anti-terrorism policies. Assuming a lag period in the LPR cycles allows the benefit of discovering trends using federal statistics that may be both widely accessible and reliable for additional research projects. Thus, in addition to the trends discovered, these data offered unbiased figures that indicated changes, namely the number of pre and post-9/11 LPRs approved by both region and category.

An Apt Selection of Terms

For the document analysis, it was a challenge to ensure the search terms used were broad enough to include all types of immigrants but also succinct enough identify relevant articles. The selection of the term "foreign-born" for the document analyses was therefore chosen for several reasons. First, any person born in a foreign country that legally seeks citizenship or permanent residency is by definition an immigrant. Using the foreign reference purposefully targets those that may be seen as "outsiders" even if eventually they are legally granted citizenship or permanent residence status. Essentially, the foreign designation instantly indicates the potential for labeling as "outsider"; which in moral panic terms, gives the prospect of becoming part of an identifiable *folk devil* population.

With regard to criminalizing particular types of immigrants or designating them as *folk devils*, Doty (2003) suggests that,

> [T]he various practice of marking one's territory does not necessarily result in clearer more secure borders. Rather it effects the designation of enemies and the marginalization and repression of certain peoples. (p. 38)

Thus, assigning labels to particular categories of people and adding specific descents or ethnic groups effectively criminalized immigrants from some geographical regions (i.e.

U.S. born of Mexican descent, foreign-born citizen, or Arab-American) even if they had gained full citizenship and are in fact legal U.S. citizens. It is arguably the case that the general criminalization of immigrants in post-9/11 society has manifested because, to this day, no particular country has been formally designated or identified as the "enemy" in the "war on terror".

The Need to Expand Categories

Future investigations in this subject should include the exploration of other visa and visitor categories, such as criminal removals and deportations, further describing the number and types of immigrants and non-citizens most affected by current and future federal regulations. Examining the trends in criminal removals and deportation changes over time may also provide evidence to demonstrate the level of effectiveness of some of the PATRIOT Act's specific "war on terror" efforts. Also, given the view that "moral panic over immigrants is fueled by economic anxiety, in particular the perception that scarce jobs are being taken by foreigners" (Welch 2002: 183), the current state of the economy may have far reaching effects on the media, public opinion, and mostly employment based LPR approvals now and for several years to come. Therefore, future studies, utilizing the moral panic context to examine the governmental and public reaction to immigration as the economy is in flux, may also reveal a new negative association in media reporting that might include an increase in hostility toward immigrants purely for economic reasons and a reduction LPR approvals, especially work based LPRs, due to poor economic conditions.

Another future research endeavor that could be undertaken is an examination of visas issued per country, which may suggest that the current media profile of negatively targeted immigrant groups is seriously misguided. As immigrants from specific countries have been identified by the media as engaging in criminal activities, terrorists, or supporters of terrorist groups,

the typical terrorist profile, based in part on national origin, may
have severe defects. These defects arise from the fact that in:

> [T]he most celebrated cases to date, the defendant was a
> citizen of a nation not listed as aiding terrorism. Zacarias
> Moussaoui, the so-called twentieth hijacker, is a French
> citizen; Richard Reid, caught with a shoe bomb he was
> trying to light on an airplane, is a British citizen; José
> Padilla, aka Abdullah Al Muhajir, accused of plotting to
> create a "dirty" or radiological bomb, is a U.S. citizen of
> Puerto Rican descent. (Welch 2003: 6)

Interestingly, two of the "war of terror" defendants hail from
countries with historically high numbers of immigrants accepted
into the U.S. and the third was actually a U.S. citizen, though in
most post-9/11 reporting, each was further identified as being of
foreign descent. This type of discovery can only further
illustrate the fact that "terrorist profiling" may contribute
erroneously to the criminalization of particular immigrant groups
in U.S. society.

The Benefit of Time and Experience

Although this study is limited to a ten-year span, future studies
of fifteen to twenty year increments, should be conducted as
trends developing from terrorist attacks or similar events in
other nations might have some effect on the sentiment and
opinions of the American public, with regard to foreigners
entering the country and U.S. immigration regulations. This
study remains significant however, as the immediate
examination of moral panics and the criminalization of
immigrants may offer some insight into the current climate that
exists in post-September 11th U.S. society. As the PATRIOT
Act continues to be modified, new legislation on illegal
migration still being formulated, and the current federal
administration is beginning to assemble its own strategy for a
reformed immigration policy, it will be interesting to observe

whether or not moral panics continue to plague the issue of immigration in the near and also distant future.

Although society has generally relaxed many of the immediate restrictions imposed as a result of terrorist activity and returned to most of its pre-9/11 social conditions, it is evident that the widespread sentiment towards immigration is currently at an impasse. As is often the case, left in the wake of moral panic is the potential for lasting social conditions and additional panics towards immigration that are affected by formal social controls and supported by informal social controls, recurring in an intermittent and episodic fashion. Currently, with the looming legislation targeting illegal migrants and recent dialogue contemplating changes to the NAFTA and other legal immigration policies, the panic against immigration may again become markedly apparent. Although the focus may shift away from its initial basis that was rooted in terrorism, U.S. society must find some solution to the continuing dilemma of establishing and managing an effective and proficient immigration system, while retaining the benefits that immigration has historically brought, and continues to bring, to U.S. society.

References

Ackerman, Bruce. 2004. "The Emergency Constitution". *Yale Law Journal* 113: 1029-1091.

Adelman, Howard. 2004. "Governance, Immigration Policy, and Security: Canada and the United States Post 9/11". Pp. 109 – 130 in *The Maze of Fear: Security and Migration after 9/11*, edited by John Tirman. New York, NY: The New Press.

Altheide, David L. 2002. *Creating Fear: News and the Construction of Crisis*. New York: Aldine de Gruyter.

Ashar, Sameer M. 2002. "Immigration Enforcement and Subordination: The Consequences of Racial Profiling After September 11". *Connecticut Law Review* 34: 1185-1199.

Baerveldt, Chris, Hans Bunkers, Micha De Winter, and Jan Kooistra. 1998. "Assessing a Moral Panic Relating to Crime and Drugs Policy in the Netherlands: Towards a Testable Theory". *Crime, Law & Social Change* 29: 31-47.

Barak, Gregg. 1994. "Media, Society, and Criminology". Pp. 3-48 in *Media, Process, and the Social Construction of Crime*, edited by Gregg Barak. New York: Garland Publishing, Inc.

Batalova, Jeanne and Alicia Lee. 2012. "US in Focus: Frequently Requested Statistics on Immigrants and Immigration in the United States". *Migration Policy Institute*, March 2012. Retrieved from: http://www.migrationinformation.org/usfocus/display.cfm?ID=886#9a

Becker, Howard S. 1963. *Outsiders: Studies in the Sociology of Deviance*. New York, NY: The Free Press of Glencoe.

Berry, Bonnie. 2004. "Right-Wing Ideology, Terrorism, and the False Promise of Security". Pp. 155-172 in *Terrorism and Counter-*

Terrorism: Criminological Perspectives, edited by Mathieu
   Deflem. Oxford, UK: Elsevier Science.
Bertram, Eva, Morris Blachman, Kenneth Sharpe, and Peter Andreas.
   1996. *Drug War Politics: The Price of Denial*. Berkeley and Los
   Angeles, CA: University of California Press.
Bischoff, Henry. 2002. *Immigration Issues*. Westport, CT: Greenwood
   Press.
Black, Donald. 1976. *The Behavior of Law*. New York, NY: Academic
   Press.
------. 1998. *The Social Structure of Right and Wrong*. Revised edition.
   San Diego, CA: Academic Press.
------. 2004. "Terrorism as Social Control". Pp. 9-18 in *Terrorism and
   Counter-Terrorism: Criminological Perspectives*, edited by
   Mathieu Deflem. Oxford, UK: Elsevier Science.
Bonn, Scott A. 2011. "How an Elite-Engineered Moral Panic Led to the
   U.S. War on Iraq". *Critical Criminology* 19:227–249.
Burns, Robert and Charles Crawford. 1999. "School Shootings, the
   Media, and Public Fear: Ingredients for a Moral Panic". *Crime,
   Law & Social Change* 32: 147-168.
Bush, George W. 2001. Address to a Joint Session of Congress and the
   American People delivered at the United States Capitol,
   Washington, D.C., September 20, 2001. Online at:
   http://www.whitehouse.gov/news/releases/2001/09/20010920-
   8.html
Cainkar, Louise. 2004. "The Impact of the September 11th Attacks on
   Arab and Muslim Community in the United States". Pp. 215-239
   in *The Maze of Fear: Security and Migration after 9/11*, edited by
   John Tirman. New York: The New Press.
Chang, Nancy. 2002. *Silencing Political Dissent*. New York: Seven
   Stories Press.
Chermak, Steven. 2004. "Crime in the News Media: A Redefined
   Understanding of How Crimes Become News". Pp. 95-130 in
   Media, Process, and the Social Construction of Crime, edited by
   Gregg Barak. New York: Garland Publishing, Inc.
Clark, William A. V. 2003. *Immigrants and the American Dream:
   remaking the Middle Class*. New York: The Guilford Press.
Clymer, Adam. 1986. "Public Found Ready to Sacrifice in Drug Fight".
   New York Times, September 2, AI: EV.

Cohen, Stanley. 1972. *Folk Devils and Moral Panics: The Creation of the Mods and Rockers*. London: MacGibbons & Kee.

------. 1985. *Visions of Social Control: Crime, Punishment and Classification*. Cambridge, MA: Polity Press.

Cole, David. 2002. "Enemy Aliens". *Stanford Law Review* 54: 953-1004.

------. 2003. "The New McCarthyism: Repeating History in the War on Terrorism". *Harvard Rights-Civil Liberties Law Review* 38: 1-30.

Cole, David. 2004. "The Priority of Morality: The Emergency Constitution's Blind Spot". *Yale Law Journal* 113: 1753-1800.

Collins, Jennifer M. 2002. "And the Walls Came Tumbling Down: Sharing Grand Jury Information with the Intelligence Community Under the USA PATRIOT Act". *American Criminal Law Review* 39: 1261-1286.

Crawford, Neta C. 2004. "The Road to Global Empire: The Logic of U.S. Foreign Policy After 9/11". *Orbis* 48(4): 685-703.

Critcher, Chas. 2003. *Moral Panics and the Media*. Philadelphia, PA: Open University Press.

Cullen, Francis T. 1984. *Rethinking Crime and Deviance Theory*. Totowa, NJ: Rowman & Allanheld.

Davis, Nannette J. and Bo Anderson. 1983. *Social Control: The Production of Deviance in the Modern State*. New York: Irvington Publishers, Inc.

Deflem, Mathieu. 2004. "Introduction: Towards a Criminological Sociology of Terrorism and Counter-Terrorism". Pp. 1-6 in *Terrorism and Counter-Terrorism: Criminological Perspectives*, edited by Mathieu Deflem. Oxford, UK: Elsevier Science.

Diaz, Jr., Jesse. 2011. "Immigration Policy, Criminalization and the Growth of the Immigration Industrial Complex: Restriction, Expulsion, and Eradication of Undocumented in the U.S." Western *Criminology Review* 12(2):35-54.

Doty, Roxanne Lynn. 2003. *Anti-Immigrantism in Western Democracies: Statecraft, Desire, and the Politics of Exclusion*. New York, NY: Routledge.

Duffy, Michael. 2003. "Could it happen Again?", *Time*, August 4, 2003.

Engel, Karen. 2004. "Constructing Good Aliens and Good Citizens: Legitimizing the War on Terror(ism)". *Colorado Law Review* 75: 59-114.

Falk, Richard A. 2003. "The Aftermath of 9/11 and the Search for Limits: In Defense of Just War Thinking".Pp. 216-222 in *The New Global Terrorism: Characteristics, Causes, Controls*, edited by Charles W. Kegley, Jr. Upper Saddle River, NJ: Prentice Hall.

Federal Bureau of Investigation. 2001. *"Terrorism ²⁰⁰⁰/2001"*. 2001. United States Department of Justice, Federal Bureau of Investigation Publication #0308. Available online at http://www.fbi.gov/publications/terror/terror2000_2001.htm.

Garland, David. 2001. *The Culture of Control: Crime and Social Order in Contemporary Society*. Chicago, IL: University of Chicago Press.

Gellman, Susan. 2002. "The First Amendment in a Time that Tries Men's Souls". *Law and Contemporary Problems* 65(2): 87-101.

Gerstle, Gary. 2004. "The Immigrant as a Threat to American Security: A Historical Perspective". Pp. 87-108 in *The Maze of Fear: Security and Migration after 9/11*, edited by John Tirman. New York: The New Press.

Glassner, Barry. 1999. *The Culture of Fear: Why Americans are Afraid of the Wrong Things*. New York, NY: Basic Books.

Goode, Erich and Nachman Ben-Yehuda. 1994. *Moral Panics: The Social Construction of Deviance*. Cambridge, MA: Blackwell.

Gusfield, Joseph R. 1967. "Moral Passage: The Symbolic Process in Public Designations of Deviance". *Social Problems* 15(2): 175-188.

Guskin, Jane and David L. Wilson. 2007. *The Politics of Immigration: Questions and Answers*. New York, NY: Monthly Review Press.

Hall, Matthew R. 2002. "Procedural Due Process Meets National Security: The Problem of Classified Evidence in Immigration Proceedings". *Cornell International Law Journal* 35: 515-532.

Haque, M. Shamsul. 2003. "Patriotism versus Imperialism". *Peace Review* 15(4): 451-456.

Hawdon, James E. 2001. "The Role of Presidential Rhetoric in the Creation of a Moral Panic: Reagan, Bush, and the War on Drugs". *Deviant Behavior: An Interdisciplinary Journal* 22: 419-445.

Hayes, Helene. 2001. U.S. *Immigration Policy and the Undocumented: Ambivalent Laws, Furtive Lives*. Westport, CT: Praeger.

Heymann, Philip B. 2002. "Civil Liberties and Human Rights in the Aftermath of September 11". *Harvard Journal of Law & Public Policy* 25: 441-456.

Hier, Sean P. 2002a. "Conceptualizing Moral Panic through a Moral Economy of Harm". *Critical Sociology* 28(3): 311-334.

------. 2002b. "Raves, Risks and the Ecstasy Panic: A Case Study in the Subversive Nature of Moral Regulation". *Canadian Journal of Sociology* 27(1): 33-57.

Holsti, Ole R. 1996. *Public Opinion and American Foreign Policy*. Ann Arbor, MI: University of Michigan Press.

Hood. M.V., III and Irwin L. Morris. 1998. "Give Us Your Tired, Your Poor,...But Make Sure They Have a Green Card: The Effects of Documented and Undocumented Migrant Context on Anglo Opinion Toward Immigration". *Political Behavior* 20(1): 1-15.

Isbister, John. 1996. *Immigration Debate: Remaking America*. West Hartford, CT: Kumarian Press, Inc.

Jensen, Eric L., Jurg Gerber, and Ginna Babcock .1991. "The New War on Drugs: Grass Roots Movement or Political Construction?". *Journal of Drug Issues* 21(3): 651-667 EV.

Kappeler, Victor E. and Aaron E. Kappeler. 2004. "Speaking of Evil and Terrorism: The Political and Ideological Construction of a Moral Panic". Pp. 175-197 in *Terrorism and Counter-Terrorism: Criminological Perspectives*, edited by Mathieu Deflem. Oxford, UK: Elsevier Science.

Katz, Karen. 2011. "The Enemy Within: The Outlaw Motorcycle Gang Moral Panic". American Journal of Criminal Justice 36(3): 231-249.

Kearney, Richard. 1999. "Aliens and Others: Between Girard and Derrida". *Cultural Values* 3(3): 251-62.

Kettl, Donald F. 2004. *System Under Stress: Homeland Security and American Politics*. Washington, DC: CQ Press.

Kitsuse, John I. 1962. "Societal Reaction to Deviant Behavior: Problems of Theory and Method". *Social Problems* 9(3): 247-256.

Klegley, Jr. ,Charles W., ed. 2003. *The New Global Terrorism: Characteristics, Causes, Controls*. Upper Saddle River, NJ: Prentice Hall.

Klinger, David A. and Dave Grossman. 2002. "Who Should Deal with Foreign Terrorists on U.S. Soil?: Socio-legal Consequences of September 11 and the Ongoing Threat of Terrorist Attacks in America". *Harvard Journal of Law & Public Policy* 25: 815-834.

Kuzma, Lynn M. 2004. "Security versus Liberty: 9/11 and the American Public". Pp. 160-190 in *The Politics of Terror: The U.S. Response to 9/11,* edited by William Crotty. Boston, MA: Northeastern University Press.

Lebowitz, Lawrence M. and Ira L. Podheiser. 2002. "A Summary of the Changes in Immigration Policies and Practices After the Terrorist Attacks of September 11, 2001: The USA PATRIOT Act and Other Measures". *University of Pittsburgh Law Review* 63: 873-888.

Lee, Kenneth K. 1998. *Huddled Masses, Muddled Laws: Why Contemporary Immigration Policy Fails to Reflect Public Opinion.* Westport, CT: Praeger.

Lemert, C. Charles and Michael F. Winter, eds. 2000. *Crime and Deviance: Essays and Innovations of Edwin M. Lemert.* New York, NY: Rowman & Littlefield Publishers, Inc.

Lemert, Edwin M. 1964. "Social Structure, Social Control, and Deviation". Pp. 57-97 in *Anomie and Deviant Behavior: A Discussion and Critique*, edited by Marshall B. Clinard. London: The Free Press of Glencoe.

Lyon, David. 2003. *Surveillance after September 11*. Cambridge, UK: Polity Press.

Malkin, Michelle. 2006. "Stricter Immigration policy is Essential to the War on Terror". Pp. 97-104 in *Illegal Immigration*, edited by Margaret Haerens. Farmington Hills, MI: Greenhaven Press.

Martin, Kate. 2004. "Domestic Intelligence and Civil Liberties". *SAIS Review* 24(1): 7-21.

McCulloch, Jude. 2002. "'Either You Are With Us or You Are With the Terrorists': The War's Home Front". Pp. 54-58 in *Beyond September 11: An Anthology of Dissent*, edited by Phil Scranton. Sterling, VA: Pluto Press.

McKenzie, April. 2004. "A Nation of Immigrants or a Nation of Suspects? State and Local Law Enforcement of Federal Immigration Laws Since 9/11". *Alabama Law Review* 55: 1149-1165.

McLean, Scott L. 2004. "The War on Terrorism and the New Patriotism". Pp. 64-94 in *The Politics of Terror: The U.S. Response to 9/11,* edited by William Crotty. Boston, MA: Northeastern University Press.

McRobbie, Angela and Sarah L. Thornton. 1995. "Rethinking 'Moral Panic' for Multi-Mediated Social Worlds". *The British Journal of Sociology* 46(4): 559-574.

Meyers, Eytan. 2004. *International Immigration Policy: A Theoretical and Comparative Analysis.* New York: Palgrave Macmillan.

Monger, Randall and James Yankay. 2012. "U.S. Legal Permanent Residents: 2011". *Annual Flow Report*, April 2012. Retrieved from: http://www.dhs.gov/xlibrary/assets/statistics/publications/lpr_fr_20 11.pdf

Morgan, George, Selda Dagistanli, and Greg Martin. 2010. "Global Fears, Local Anxiety: Policing, Counterterrorism and Moral Panic Over 'Bikie Gang Wars' in New South Wales." *Australian & New Zealand Journal of Criminology* 43(3): 580-599.

Mukherjee, Roopali. 2003. Between Enemies and Traitors: Black Press Coverage of September 11 and the Predicaments of National "Others". Pp. 29–46 in *Media Representations of September 11th,* edited by Steven Chermak, Frankie Y. Bailey, and Michelle Brown. Westport, CT: Praeger Publishers.

New York Times. 2001. "The War against America: An Unfathomable Attack". *New York Times*, September 12, 2001, Late Edition - Final, Section A; Column 1; Editorial Desk; Pg. 26

Newman, Deborah Wilkins. 2003. "September 11: A Societal Reaction Perspective". *Crime, Law & Social Change* 39:219-231.

Nguyen, Tram. 2005. *We are All Suspects Now: Untold Stories from Immigrant Communities After 9/11.* Boston, MA: Beacon Press.

Orcutt, James D. and J. Blake Turner. 1993. "Shocking Numbers and Graphic Accounts: Quantified Images of Drug Problems in the Print Media". *Social Problems* 40(2): 190-206.

Paletz, David L. and Robert M. Entman. 1981. *Media Power Politics.* New York: The Free Press.

Parenti, Michael. 2002. *The Terrorism Trap: September 11 and Beyond.* San Francisco, CA: City Lights Books.

Pew, Global Attitudes Project. (2001) . "Post September 11 attitudes". *The PEW Research Center for the People and the Press*. Retrieved on April 14, 2009 from http://people-press.org/reports/pdf/144.pdf

Pijpers, Roos. 2006. "Help! The Poles are Coming: Narrating a Contemporary Moral Panic". *Geografiska Annaler* 88 B(1): 91-103.

Pound, Roscoe. [1942] 1997. *Social Control Through Law*. New Brunswick, NJ: Transaction Publishers.

------. 1943. "A Survey of Social Interests". *Harvard Law Review* 57(1): 1-39.

Quinney, Richard. 1970. *The Social Reality of Crime*. Boston, MA: Little, Brown and Company.

Reimers, David M. 1998. *Unwelcome Strangers: American Identity and the Turn Against Immigration*. New York, NY: Columbia University Press.

Rothe, Dawn and Stephen L. Muzzatti. 2004. "Enemies Everywhere: Terrorism, Moral Panic, and US Civil Society". *Critical Criminology* 12: 327-350.

Saux, Maria Soledad. 2007. "Immigration and Terrorism: A Constructed Connection". *European Journal of Crime and Policy Research* 13:57-72.

Scheuerman, William E. 2002. "Rethinking Crisis Government". *Constellations* 9(4): 492-505.

Shutt, J. Eagle, and Mathieu Deflem. 2005. "Whose Face at the Border? Homeland Security and Border Policing Since 9/11". *Journal of Social and Ecological Boundaries* 1(2):81-105.

Slevin, Peter and Mary Beth Sheridan. 2001. "Suspects Entered U.S. on Legal Visas". *Washington Post*, September 18: A06.

Slone, Michelle and Anat Shoshani. 2010. "Prevention Rather than Cure? Primary or Secondary Intervention for Dealing with Media Exposure to Terrorism". *Journal of Counseling & Development* 88(4):440-448.

Smith, Brent L. 1994. *Terrorism in America: Pipe Bombs and Pipe Dreams*. Albany, NY: State University of New York Press.

Smith, Brian. 2005. "Another Step Away from Full Due Process Protections". *Akron Law Review* 38: 207-252.

The Associated Press State & Local Wire. 2001. "Foreign-born Mainers Differ on Inquiries". December 9, Sunday, BC cycle.

------. 2003. "FBI Agent Says Terrorism Still a Threat in Oklahoma". March 30, Sunday, BC cycle.

Thomas, Philip A. 2002. "Legislative Responses to Terrorism". Pp. 93-101 in *Beyond September 11: An Anthology of Dissent,* edited by Phil Scranton. Sterling, VA: Pluto Press.

Thompson, Kenneth. 1998. *Moral Panics.* New York: Routledge.

Timms, Ed. 2004. "'First Responders' Find Their Jobs Even Tougher", The Dallas Morning News, September 12, 2003. Pp 37-40 in *Homeland Security, The Reference Shelf,* 76(1), edited by Norris Smith and Lynn M. Messina. Bronx, NY: H.W. Wilson Company.

Ting, Jan. 2003. "Immigration Law Reform After 9/11: What Has Been and What Still Needs to Be Done". *Temple International and Comparative Law Journal* 17: 503-521.

Turk, Austin T. 2004. "Sociology of Terrorism". *Annual Review of Sociology 30*: 271-286.

Ungar, Sheldon 2001. "Moral Panic Versus the Risk Society: The Implications of the Changing Sites of Social Anxiety". *British Journal of Sociology* 52(2): 279-291.

United States Department of Justice. 2001: "Life and Liberty". Available online at: http://www.lifeandliberty.gov.

Uniting and Strengthening America by Providing Appropriate Tools Required to Intercept and Obstruct Terrorism (USA PATRIOT Act) Act of 2001. Passed October 24, 2001, H.R. 3162 RDS, 107th Congress, 1st Session. Available online at: http://www.epic.org/privacy/terrorism/hr3162.html

Waddington, P.A.J. 1986. "Mugging as a Moral Panic: A Question of Proportion". *The British Journal of Sociology* 37(2): 245-259.

Wanta, W., Golan, G., & Lee, C. (2004). "Agenda setting and international news: Media influence on public perceptions of foreign nations". *Journalism and Mass Communication Quarterly,* 81, 364–377.

Ward, Russell E., Jr. 2002. "Fan Violence: Social Problem or Moral Panic?". Aggression and Violent Behavior (7): 453-475.

Welch, Michael. 2000. *Flag Burning: Moral Panic and the Criminalization of Protest.* New York: de Gruyter

------. 2002. *Detained: Immigration Laws and the Expanding I.N.S. Jail Complex.* Philadelphia, PA: Temple University Press.

------. 2003. "Trampling Human Rights in the War on Terror: Implications to the Sociology of Denial". *Critical Criminology* (12): 1-20.

------. 2006a. "Seeking a safer society: America's anxiety in the war on terror". *Security Journal*, 19, 93–109.

------. 2006b. *Scapegoats of September 11th*. Piscataway, NJ: Rutgers University Press.

White, John Kenneth. 2004. "Terrorism and the Remaking of American Politics". Pp. 37-63 in *The Politics of Terror: The U.S. Response to 9/11*, edited by William Crotty. Boston, MA: Northeastern University Press.

Whitehead, John W. and Steven H. Aden. 2002. "Forfeiting 'Enduring Freedom' for 'Homeland Security': A Constitutional Analysis if the USA PATRIOT Act and the Justice Department's Anti-Terrorism Initiatives". *The American Law Review* 51: 1081-1133.

Young, Jock. 1971. "The Role of Police as Amplifiers of Deviance, Negotiators of Drug Control as Seen in Notting Hill". Pp. 27-61 in *Images of Deviance*, edited by Stanley Cohen. Harmondsworth, England: Penguin Books.

------. 2009. "Moral Panic: Its Origins in Resistance, Ressentiment and the Translation of Fantasy into Reality". *The British Journal of Criminology* 49(1): 4-16.

Zinn, Howard. 2002. *Terrorism and War*. New York: Seven Stories Press.

Zucconi, Mario. 2004. "Migration and Security as an Issue in U.S.-European Relations". Pp. 142-154 in *The Maze of Fear: Security and Migration after 9/11*, edited by John Tirman. New York: The New Press.

Index

CPSIA information can be obtained at www.ICGtesting.com
Printed in the USA
LVOW06*1448110514

385311LV00004B/22/P